Agora Borealis | Engaging in Sustainable Architecture

Vivian Manasc & Cheryl Mahaffy

Partners In Design Books

A Partners In Design book

Published by: Partners in Design Books
                     an imprint of The Books Collective
                     214-21, 10405 Jasper Avenue
                     Edmonton, Alberta, Canada T5J 3S2

Partners In Design Books is an imprint created by the Sustainable Design Consortium. For information about the other activities of the Consortium, please write c/o 10225 100 Avenue Edmonton AB Canada T5J 0A1.

The Books Collective acknowledges the support of the Canada Council for the Arts, the Alberta Foundation for the Arts, and the Edmonton Arts Council for our publishing programme. Partners in Design Books further acknowledges the support of the Sustainable Design Consortium.

Consulting editors: Candas Jane Dorsey and Timothy J. Anderson
Cover and interior design: Anna Coe
Photo credits see page 172
Interior typeset by Anna Coe in Mrs. Eaves, a classic and warm typeface reminscent of letterpress printing, designed by Zuzana Licko in 1996, Bodoni, recognized by its highly contrasting strokes, pure vertical stress, and hairline serifs, designed by Morris Fuller Benton between 1908–1915 and Myriad designed by Robert Slimbach & Carol Twombly with Fred Brady & Christopher Slye, acknowledged for its warmth and readability resulting from a humanistic treatment of letter proportions.
Thanks to Don Becker, Derek Heslop, Milan Krepelka, Jack McCutcheon, Raoul Mendoza, Myron Nebozuk and Wes Sims.
Printed in Canada on 70lb Reincarnation Matte text, which is 50 percent post—consumer waste and 100 percent recycled and a Cornwall C1S 10pt cover by Priority Printing. Thanks to Kim Lundquist.

1 2 3 4 5 06 05 04 03 02

National Library of Canada Cataloguing in Publication Data

Manasc, Vivian, 1956-
   Agora borealis

Copublished by: Sustainable Buildings Consortium.
Includes bibliographical references.
ISBN 1-894880-01-3

   1. Architecture--Environmental aspects--Canada. 2. Architecture and climate--Canada. I. Mahaffy, Cheryl, 1955- II. Sustainable Buildings Consortium. III. Title.
NA2542.35.M36 2002   720'.47   C2002-910880-2

CONTENTS

agora n. Gk. Hist. an assembly
or place of assembly, esp.
a marketplace. (Greek)

boreal adj. 1 of the North or
northern regions. 2 of the north
wind. (Middle English from
French *boréal* or Late Latin
borealis from Latin *Boreas*
from Greek Boreas god of
the north wind)

engage b. attract and hold fast
(a person's attention, interest,
etc.) c. draw (a person) into a
conversation.

The story in brief.

Manasc Isaac Architects of Edmonton, Alberta has committed its team to charting a sustainable course amid the vagaries of Canada's northern climate. Out of that journey are emerging early incarnations of the agora needed in the north, but also around the globe: long-lasting, community friendly, occupant friendly, energy efficient structures whose operating costs demonstrate that so-called green architecture can bring financial as well as environmental rewards. Equally important are lessons learned along the way about process, and especially about the paradigm shift required to create these buildings: a shift to the full-scale integration that ponders each decision in light of its impact on the whole.

Agora Borealis makes the case for sustainable building by taking readers behind the scenes, telling how and why four Manasc Isaac structures came to be. This is a story of targets set and (usually) met, of energy (generally) saved, of tenants (mostly) comfortable in their space and of people, occupants and communities engaged in the design of their environments. It's a story of turning theory into a reality that performs increasingly better than the norm. Most of all, it's a story of the teams, attitudes and materials behind a new and evolving generation of buildings. By sharing the Manasc Isaac journey as story, warts included, this book aims to squelch myths and inspire imitation, thus advancing ability that is crucial to our collective future.

The buildings highlighted here directly contradict the most stubborn and obstructive myth of all: the belief that sustainable buildings cost far too much, and benefit little. Here we see buildings whose strong lines, occupant comforts and confirmed cost-benefit records confirm that sustainability makes sense. Even (or perhaps especially) in the north, where particular skill is required to ride rather than battle elemental extremes.

In the spotlight.

- **Banff Town Hall,**
  which kindled the desire to accomplish more,
  while demonstrating the complexities involved;

- **Hinton Government Centre,**
  which draws air, light (indeed, the bulk of its energy)
  from immediate surroundings;

- **Intuit Canada headquarters,**
  whose energizing ambiance grows in part from an
  innovative mix of windows, wood and worker amenities;

- **Amiskwaciy Academy,**
  which reincarnates Edmonton's mothballed Municipal
  Airport Terminal as a First Nations high school.

As in all good stories, what transpires as real-world projects take shape includes moments of falling as well as rising action. Times when plans go awry, when timelines limit opportunities. Such moments demand telling, for they hold potential to inform others intent on plotting this same path. Equally important, this story isn't complete; much more remains to be learned about sustainable design for northern climates. Insights gained by creating and operating today's sustainable buildings and increasingly creating sustainable communities will spawn an advanced generation of life-enhancing structures, built for the long term.

sustainable 1. Ecology (esp. of development) that conserves an ecological balance by avoiding depletion of natural resources. 2. that may be maintained, esp. at a particular level.

architecture (n) a. the art or science of designing and constructing buildings. 3. buildings or other structures collectively.

Tweaking interest.

Cheryl: My first introduction to Vivian Manasc and her work came in an e-mail from Alberta Venture publisher Ruth Kelly, for whom I'd written a succession of complex, research-intensive articles. "How about an easier piece like we've been promising you?" wrote Ruth, adding that she'd recently met a woman who'd make "a fascinating article," an architect originally from Romania and schooled in Montreal who'd headed west decades ago in pursuit of opportunity. "She's built a firm, with some adversity, and is very passionate about architecture, in particular for environmentally healthy buildings," Ruth continued. "She is the brains behind the Sustainable Buildings Symposium, which is held annually. I think you'd like her. Does it tweak your interest?"

Little did I expect that the resulting profile of Vivian Manasc would lead to the book you hold, a project that makes some of those earlier articles seem a snap. Soon after the profile hit the street in March 2001, Vivian called to say its style fit a story she wanted to tell—the story of her journey into sustainable architecture. She'd like to team up on a book, or as she later termed it, a storybook. A work that might inspire others to undertake their own journeys. Did it tweak my interest?

No question. My brief dip into her world told me that Vivian Manasc has reason to be passionate about environmentally healthy buildings and about an even broader scope of work that she calls sustainable architecture through integrated building design. I'd seen enough to be convinced that, unless this radically different approach to putting buildings together spreads like aurora borealis in a northern sky, we can set aside hope of stalling climate change and hitting Kyoto targets. After all, as I'd discovered in surfing for statistics, up to half of the energy consumed worldwide is used to construct and operate buildings. Architects such as Vivian are proving that a dedicated team focused on sustainability can significantly shrink that appetite, beating today's energy benchmarks by fifty percent with little if any increase in construction cost while refining numerous other building parameters, from indoor air quality to longevity.

Yet those architects shape but a handful of the structures popping out of farmers' fields and urban parking lots, particularly in places like booming Alberta. In a business where mistakes can cost millions, it's all too easy to follow old paradigms.

I realized that the winds of change are blocked in the northern marketplace not only by economics and inertia, but by persistent myths rooted in so-called green buildings of the past—those costly, ugly, light-deprived boxes that, quite frankly, make people sick. You may remember the shrunken windows of the '70s from your own school days; perhaps you're living or working in one of today's sealed boxes. In the structures designed by Vivian and the crew at Manasc Isaac Architects, by contrast, I saw pleasing lines, occupant comforts and (best of all, in my view) large, opening windows.

"Innovation flourishes in greenhouses. What do I mean by greenhouses? A place where the elements are just right to foster the growth of good ideas. Where there's heat, light, moisture, and plenty of nurturing. The greenhouse we're talking about, of course, is the workplace, the way spaces take shape in offices and teams work together." *~Tom Kelly with Jonathan Littman*

In the teams behind those buildings, meanwhile, I heard enthusiasm fueled by results that equal or even outperform theoretical models, coupled with determination to set the bar even higher. Not that these teams have figured everything out, or agree on all the right approaches, or keep tenants happy 100 percent of the time. But they are engaged in a journey that adds new meaning and purpose to their work. And they love to tell the story.

"If you want understanding, you have to re—enter the human world of stories...I don't mean fiction or stories heavy with plot; I mean narrative that string events together in time and shows them unfolding." *~David Weinberger*

That, in essence, is how sustainable building will spread through agora borealis, the northern marketplace; how it is spreading, albeit too slowly: through buildings like those described in these pages, and the stories of how they came to be. This paradigm shift has got to happen. Does it tweak your interest? Read on.

"In the past we could afford a long gestation period before undertaking major environmental policy initiatives. Today the time for a well-planned transition to a sustainable system is running out. We may be moving in the right direction, but we are moving too slowly. We are failing in our responsibility to future generations and even the present one."

~Kofi Annan, U.N. Secretary-General, 2001

"A whole is defined by the pattern of relations between it's parts, not by the sum of its parts: And a civilization is not defined by the sum of its science, technology, art, and social organization, but by the total pattern which they form, and the degree of harmonious integration in that pattern." ~Arther Koestler

"Talk that lasts is about stuff we can't stop talking about.

In other words, what makes the most meaningful ideas

combustible is also what makes them inextinguishable. In

modern parlance, enduring ideas are viral memes: social

DNA that constantly evolves, raising collective consciousness

through conversation that can only grow. Democracy,

mathematics, and politics are all viral memes that were born

in the agora, the Greek marketplace." ~*Doc Searls*

Playback.

Vivian: It took me a long time to understand the gift of telling stories—and the importance of stories in the architectural design process. Perhaps our 1990 work to build a school in Saddle Lake best illustrates how this particular insight came, gradually and through story.

I had initiated a community involvement process with the Saddle Lake First Nation, holding numerous workshops to hear the individual and collective visions for this new school. Through the many months of design, we had worked with elders, children, politicians, teachers, parents, administrators. The design that emerged, representing the form of an eagle, was based on consultation and the vision of Noah Cardinal, the school's resident Elder. To that point, the stories were secondary, just enough to feed our limited understanding and insight.

Then Diane Steinhauer joined the team as director of education. A young educator originally from Saddle Lake, Diane had just returned to her roots and was keen to see the school in operation. As she started to talk about the stories embodied in the school, the image of the eagle took on new depth. She shared aspects of the eagle child story, describing how the eagle child had traveled to the four directions seeking wisdom and insight — only to find those back at the start of the journey.

Diane suggested Stewart Steinhauer be commissioned to create a symbolic sculpture for the centre of the school, but we needed more. As the schools' meaning became more layered, stories needed to be told. Some suggested murals or other ways of telling those stories, but elders advised that the stories belong to an oral tradition. Not really intended to be written or told literally, these stories had to be interpreted in a more subtle and abstract way. At the time, I was designing the interior of the school. Thinking the linoleum floor could be the keeper of its story, I asked Diane to find me the story so I could interpret it.

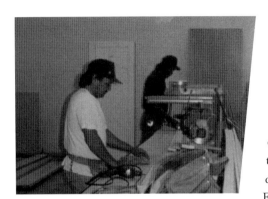

At Saddle Lake, local residents skilled and apprenticing in various trades constructed ninety percent of the school and more recent healing center. Since then, many projects – including schools at Peguis, Driftpile and O'Chiese, a health centre and RCMP building at Peigan, a new health facility in the Athabasca Basin – benefited from significant proportions of local work. Typically, eighty percent or more of the construction on these First Nations buildings is completed by community residents.

Not nearly so simple, I discovered. We had to go and ask for the story from Peter O'Chiese, one of the traditional elders. In a ceremony at his home by Lac St. Anne, we were given the gift of a story to interpret. Thus it was that we integrated the story of the seven stages of life, with its complexities, subtleties and meanings, into the story of the eagle child—and interpreted both stories in the detailed design of the new school at Saddle Lake. The school's colourful floor pattern carries the essence of the story, which can be told and re-told by successive generations of elders, teachers and students.

Curiosity drove me to explore further. I love the idea that stories can be hidden and layered into the design of a building and that these stories could be revealed, or not, at various times. What ideas would emerge through the vehicle of telling stories?

We started listening to the myriad stories about the making of buildings in Saddle Lake. The importance of local involvement in construction and the importance of being connected to the various threads of the design and construction began to emerge, adding to our resolve to use local expertise and labour. Once the school opened, I found myself there, one day, overhearing a conversation between two students. Each proudly claimed some credit for the building, as a father or uncle had been part of its construction.

This really was an early lesson in sustainable design. What's sustainable, I learned, is a building that is understood and rooted in its place. As Saddle Lake has since shown, such a place is not vandalized, but rather used and respected in the community.

Sustainable design as an idea, as a way to talk about what should be, appeared gradually as I worked in numerous northern and Native communities, and came to understand that building technology alone cannot achieve long-term cost-effective structures. Seeing what emerged when we integrated community into the design process. We took the next logical leap of integrating the whole design team into the process.

Or perhaps that was actually the first level. Maybe the urge to integrate the design team emerged through experience in the client's shoes.

Early in my adventure in architectural offices, I had the opportunity to write proposals. Yet I didn't know what they looked

like from the other side. What would it be like to read and evaluate the various proposals from all the city's leading firms? I was curious to find out what was in the client's mind.

Then the opportunity to be in that mind presented itself, as assistant director of design and construction at the Edmonton Public School Board. I was welcomed to the post with a revealing task: short-listing architectural firms for ten new schools. Exciting times followed, as I had the chance to create the short list, interview the architects and select the final ten. Working with those firms over the next year, I quickly realized that integration and cross-pollination of information would help maintain my sanity. Ten firms, all different, showed me aspects of architectural practice that I respected and admired—and many other aspects that I found condescending and frustrating. There was little ability to integrate client views into the design process. The engineering team's contributions were prescriptive and predictable, resulting in building systems with varying degrees of sophistication. Architectural form and function was about as far as it got in many of the projects. Still, some terrific schools came from that era, and I began to understand both the power of an effective client and the importance of an integrated design and construction team.

"Conversations...are manifest in stories of heroes, accounts of defining failures, gossip, and, of course, silently in peoples heads. Coversation is the single most important business process when the goal is to shift what people believe and how they think." ~*Surfing the Edge of Chaos*

In the end, I knew we had to create a different design process. My years at the school board gave me time to explore and tinker—to understand what worked and what didn't and to do research on group creativity and other topics that I hoped would inform a new way of designing the design process.

Those years also began the unraveling of some earlier assumptions about my profession. In the early 1980s, when I started practicing architecture, I took for granted that "energy efficiency" was a given. After all, we had lived through the energy crisis of the 1970s and knew this was clearly the way of the future. Alternative energy, solar collectors, passive solar design and earth sheltered buildings were staples of my architecture school days at McGill.

We learned to conserve energy by enclosing walls and roofs with continuous air-vapour membranes, specifying appropriate levels of insulation and designing "rainscreen" walls. Having studied architecturally integrated mechanical and electrical systems, I knew that engineers could design systems to meet any challenge, from windows that open to conditions that fluctuate wildly. "Sustainable design" as a term was not used until much later, but integrated design was certainly known and understood, at least in some places. So I assumed everyone else in the architectural and engineering and construction world understood things much as I did.

Vivian Manasc, Jeremy Sturgess and Richard Isaac worked together on the YVRC, which earned Canada's highest architectural award, the Governor General's Medal of Excellence. Completed in 1992 on the Alaska Highway at Whitehorse, it's an oasis whose exhibit hall reveals mountain views through full-height thermal glazed windows. Curved beams, exposed inside and out, define a structure whose imagery includes a tent, a kayak frame, a fish skeleton and an airplane wing. As Jeremy Sturgess says, "It's a building that belongs in that place. It wouldn't appear anywhere else."

In the late '80s, I began working with Oxford-trained Architect Richard Isaac. Attracted across the pond in 1982 by tales of the north, he moved to Wabasca (250 kilometres north of Edmonton) as a Frontier Foundation volunteer and stretched a six-month stint to long-term expatriation while building not only homes, but relationships. Soon after we joined forces, First Nations communities gained the authority to design their own schools, and we responded by inviting leaders to a workshop we called "The ABCs of School Planning." As Isaac recalls, "I thought it was a crazy idea at the time, but it turned out to be our first fumbling steps toward our design workshop format."

Although we didn't realize it at the time, decades of experience in northern communities laid an essential foundation for full scale sustainability. In our approach to northern buildings, we used leading technical strategies to create continuous and warm building envelopes, but were still designing those envelopes somewhat independently of the building systems. Designing the Yukon Visitor Centre in Whitehorse in 1991, I recall the challenge we faced in keeping the structure all on the warm side of the membrane and insulation, despite structural engineers' preference to push the structure through the envelope. We prevailed, but not without some differences in perspective. High performance glazing thermal mass and wood structures completed the technical aspects of this project, but we hadn't yet integrated our thinking about environmental impact of buildings.

Yet it wasn't until we designed the Banff Town Hall, whose story is told in the following chapter, that I really understood the extent to which many colleagues and clients were starting with assumptions that differ from mine. Although we had been systematically designing northern and extreme-climate buildings, applying consistent principles, these principles were neither well articulated nor well understood. Lacking a common language, we hadn't seized opportunities to "push the envelope" because we hadn't created a vision that would unite the entire team. The engineers basically designed as they had learned to do, demanding more space and larger duct sizes at each turn. Electrical designers had long since based lighting design levels on worst-case conditions, reasoning that it's dark outside some of the time. Given the entrenched "conventional wisdom" of building design, it was tricky to challenge unstated assumptions.

Then Banff handed us a goal too high to reach alone. Beat the Model National Energy Code by fifty percent, our client said. That's when that next level of sustainable design became an imperative: integrate the team. Without pooling our knowledge, we'd fall short of the target.

Not that integration was automatic. When we asked our engineers to integrate daylight into the design, for example, they initially thought that was interesting but not especially relevant. Everyone had designed light shelves; wasn't that all there was to it? Then we all applied ourselves to gaining a better understanding of the performance of windows, daylight patterns and patterns of light. Could we really change the type and quality of electric light by considering daylight?

Likewise, our mechanical engineers were accustomed to designing cooling systems for the hottest day of the year, sizing everything accordingly. Could we design a building so it would be comfortable most of the year? Could we design a building that wouldn't need cooling at all, reducing heat gain through careful orientation?

As we challenged assumed "must haves," the questions we asked became far more important than knowing the answers. Then energy modeling entered the scene, a new tool that could begin to generate some answers by simulating the building's performance. While still less than sophisticated, modeling improved the acceptance of new alternatives by providing factual support for design decisions.

Other First Nation school projects, including Driftpile, O'Chiese and Peguis, expanded our repertoire of community involvement strategies and deepened our understanding of the benefits won through cultural as well as technical connections to the community. The need to make these remote schools easy to maintain shaped many of the systems and also, ironically, led to one of our signature sustainable design strategies: operable windows. After all, what better backup for a ventilation system that might fail in a remote community than low-tech windows that open.

And so our journey into sustainable design is a tale with a rich weave of subplots. We focus in the next chapters on just four threads, spun as we began integrating the stories, the communities and the engineering and construction teams into the challenge of designing a new type of building. You'll hear both of our voices and the voices of a few others that have travelled so far with us.

Dozens more chapters remain to be written, by an expanding pool of authors—and I fully expect the results will soon touch all of our lives. For the best news is, this is a tale with rising action. A story that has only just begun.

Erskine's empty beauty

In the late 1970s, Ralph Erskine, a famous British/Swedish architect, designed a housing project in the Northwest Territories' Resolute Bay. This much-published project was considered the model of "sustainable," climactically and culturally sensitive design. Evocative sketches had young architects excited.

In 1988, enroute to Grise Fiord where we were designing a new health centre, I stopped in Resolute Bay. There, I heard a story about a housing project designed by a well-known architect that had long-since been boarded up. I was curious, but had no time to explore further.

The next summer, I found myself back in Resolute Bay with a group of architects and engineers, heading to a site inspection. Fogged in, we tried to fill the days until the next plane. As we walked the rocky landscape through the fog, the story of this famous housing project emerged. Designed by Ralph Erskine, fully finished and furnished with modern Swedish furniture, it had never been occupied! We drove there to check it out. Sure enough, there it was in all its splendour, much like the pictures in the magazines I had read.

With time on our hands, we pulled away the plywood barriers, crawled into an entrance and then, up a few stairs, into an apartment. After our eyes adjusted to the dim light, we could clearly make out the original Swedish furniture, the beautifully detailed and simple coat hooks, and the spartan spaces, well-suited to this northern place. All carefully designed for the "Eskimos". The building faced the sun, it was compact and efficient—and almost beautiful.

So—what happened? Why was this project abandoned before anyone ever called it home? Friends from Resolute Bay offered two theories: either the local people couldn't stand living so close together (although it made some apparent economic sense) or the plumbing lines froze and couldn't be thawed. It's hard to say which story is more believable, but this visit left a clear image of the need to connect architecture to its place. First, we cannot design sustainably until we really understand local culture; second, we cannot meet high-performance standards unless we carefully integrate building systems into overall design. Sustainable design really is a complex and layered challenge that requires attention to the vision and the detail at every level.

"It is realized that energy is a valuable, scarce and polluting resource. Building volumes must therefore become simple and heavily insulated in both hot and cold climates, thermal bridges must be minimized and windows severely restricted in size. But, controlled solar heat collection can lead to carefully oriented glass areas of considerable size. ~*Ralph Erskine, 1978*

Banff

Town

Hall

Mile Zero: Banff Town Hall escalates integration.

"Sustainable architecture." Before 1994, I might have given you a textbook definition of that term, without thinking twice about what it means for the cold-climate architect. Today, sustainability is at the heart of our design approach. Seeing is believing, as they say, and the real-time evidence of better buildings is charging the atmosphere, shifting our sense of what works. For a growing number of us, adding new structures to the landscape means not only aiming for striking facades and stunning interiors, but doing everything in our power to create long-lasting, occupant friendly, energy efficient structures that bring financial as well as environmental rewards. What's more, we are doing it together. Forming multidisciplinary teams that work in concert to create integrated structures. In the notoriously specialized and competitive world of building, that's truly a paradigm shift.

"Architecture does not typically change until the context in which it occurs changes. To design differently, to design environmentally reponsively and responsibly will require a fundamentally different view of our relation to and place within the natural world." ~Ray J. Cole

For me, it all started innocently enough, with an opportunity in one of Earth's special places: Banff National Park. Having become a self-governing municipality in 1990 after 100 years under federal rule, the Town of Banff needed a seat of government, and put out a call for proposals in late 1994. Having cut our teeth on public buildings, we had the expertise to tackle this job. But I knew we'd stand a better chance of winning the competition in partnership with Jeremy Sturgess, with whom we'd just proven our mettle on the Yukon Visitor Reception Centre. The Calgary-based Sturgess, just down the road from Banff, would add

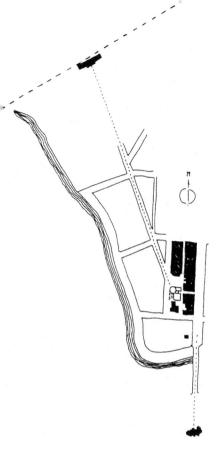

the advantage of proximity plus award-winning design sense that complements ours. A quick call to Jeremy put the wheels in motion; one busier-than-expected set of so-called Christmas "holidays" later, we submitted what turned out to be the winning proposal.

The town's proposal call mentioned a desire to participate in C-2000, a fledgling federal program offering top-up funds for commercial buildings outperforming the national energy standard by fifty percent. The request for a green building didn't surprise us. Not only is Banff part of an environmentally sensitive UNESCO World Heritage site, but its residents committed to a no-net-negative environmental impact philosophy when assuming governance of the town. Yet we didn't investigate the C-2000 program too thoroughly at the time, nor did we anticipate stretching far to meet its demands. After all, we'd worked minor miracles in the north, becoming known especially for our impermeable and sophisticated building envelopes. "We know what it is to be energy efficient," we told each other; "we'll figure out the rest." And in a way, we did. Yet I'll always remember this project as the one that taught us what more we can do. A lesson that launched us on the journey we're still traveling today.

Puzzling the pieces.

Our team put Manasc in the role of prime consultant and Sturgess in the lead for conceptual design, so Jeremy Sturgess and partner Leslie Beale stickhandled the first leg of the Banff Town Hall, crafting the building's shape and physical appearance. To anchor that work, I facilitated numerous client workshops, inviting councillors and staff to depict their vision of the space using hands-on materials such as collages and cutouts. And I teamed up with engineers Tony Grice and Chris Jepson to lead equally crucial workshops with consultants.

As Sturgess recalls, those interactive sessions quickly clarified the parameters. The town was seeking an inviting public space that would lead naturally into key legislative and administrative rooms. Squeezed onto a smallish site, the 1,555 square metre (16,7fifty square foot) building needed to relate visually to the town's historic buildings, particularly The Banff Park Museum. And it must fit within an urban plan that envisioned the town hall and the train station as anchors at opposite ends of Lynx Street, counterpoints reflecting the town's historic roots and new-found status.

Those parameters in mind, the team designed a two-storey town hall with strong wooden influences, clearly modern while evoking both local history and surrounding mountain shapes. The building embraces a sheltered public square, inviting pedestrians to stroll both outside and along a parallel interior walkway. The Mayor's Office perches above an open-sided, prow-like "beak" that overlooks an adjacent interpretive park while allowing traffic to flow underneath.

"This inspired siting for the town hall was enforced by its massing and the depostion of the plaza in front, which can provide intimacy for a ceremony for a few dozen people or serve as a venue for large civic celebrations and concerts when the street is closed." ~Trever Boddy

At the opposite end of the site, a dramatic fan-shaped Council Chamber curves around a huge birch tree that was carefully protected during construction. Connecting these wings is a two-storey administrative block whose central staircase encourages interaction and exercise rather than use of the elevator where, as Sturgess notes, "nobody talks." Surfaced in durable concrete to withstand the pound of hiking boots, the staircase became one of many nods to the huge mountain park enveloping this community of 7,000.

Concept mapped, the weight shifted north to Edmonton, where we began identifying the technical systems needed to make the building work. True to our promise, project architect Derek Heslop gathered manuals and instructions from Nils Larsson, C-2000 program manager in Ottawa. "But nobody had time to read it all in detail," he ruefully recalls. Instead, our team plowed forward mostly by seat-of-pants intuition, coupled with quick reference to pilot C-2000 buildings.

As recommended by C-2000, we used modeling software to weigh various options. But that tool proved less than sophisticated, Heslop says. "For example, the fact that we changed the domestic hot water system supposedly saved fifty percent on the water bill, yet municipal buildings use very little hot water."

"The taller mass of the administration offices to the east will shade the plaza mornings. The lower mass of the Council Chambers will admit more sunlight into the space mid-day in summer and winter. The trees planted along Bear Street to the west will shade the plaza and west elevation of the building in summer and allow sunlight in during winter. This will reduce the summer air temperature of the space in summer and raise it in winter. The raised second floor offices on the north side of the plaza will create a shaded area in summer and a sheltered sun trap in winter."
~ C-2000 Project Design Brief, 1994

With the hindsight of subsequent projects, I now realize that we brought C-2000 in as an overlay. Like so many who dip a toe into this pond, we saw sustainability as one more alligator to wrestle rather than a new way of making it to the other side. Certainly, we paid attention to critical parameters that brought success in past projects, and so we specified a high-performance envelope—a continuous, fully sealed membrane encasing the entire structure. But we took such steps because we'd built in the north, not because we were consciously rethinking the building as a whole.

Emerging integration.

Despite our overlay attitude, the need to meet C-2000's demanding standards pulled our project team toward collaboration. Crossing professional boundaries, we began to articulate connections between lighting and energy, between windows that open and indoor air quality. "We were learning how to work in an integrative fashion, which is key to the process," recalls Project Architect Derek Heslop. "We intuitively knew that was how it had to be, although it was only afterwards that people articulated that approach."

Fortunately, we were working with engineers who had a clue, including electrical engineer Tony Grice and mechanical designer Chris Jepson. Jepson's employer, Keen Engineering, had just completed the C.K. Choi Building in Vancouver, a West Coast building complete with composting toilets that proved less can definitely be better.

As Jepson recalls, success in Vancouver set the stage for similar innovation when Banff came calling. "The group of people involved came together, and looked at it from a holistic point of view. This is not what engineers usually do, but for Tony and me, who had worked with the architectural profession many years, it was an opportunity to do a little bit of thinking about each other's role."

Adds Jepson, "I could then go with less mechanical cooling, which allows a different approach. Now we can drill into the aquifer for water to cool the building. Whereas with a conventional cooling load, we would've needed a chiller instead."

Minus the need to power a chiller, Grice adds, "I was able to put in half the size of transformer. So as you see, it's a dynamic process; one element affects the other." That deliberate shrinkage of systems may seem like simple common sense, but it's the mirror opposite of today's norm, Jepson observes. "Traditionally, brighter lights demand a bigger chiller, which means a bigger transformer. It just grows."

"Business and other human endeavors are bound by invisible fabrics of interrelated actions, which often take years to fully play out their effects on each other. Since

"As architects and engineers, we've made tighter and tighter boundaries around

we are part of that lacework ourselves,

the disciplines involved in putting a building together. Sustainability blurs those

it's doubly hard to see the whole pattern

boundaries. We have to think into each other's disciplines."

of change. Instead, we tend to focus on snapshots of isolated parts of the system, and wonder why our deepest problems never seem to get solved." ~Peter Senge

And so, just as the C.K. Choi building began transforming Keen Engineering, the work on Banff became an "aha" experience for our crew. "We really saw that engineering could be a different experience," Grice says, "something where you can do a very attractive, energy efficient building, be very satisfied from a professional point of view and also maybe do something for the environment."

Indeed, our design of the Banff Town Hall promised to cut gas and electricity use in half, saving more than $10 000 a year while reducing the release of greenhouse gases and minimizing the load on power and gas utilities. We'd accomplished that by tapping the underground aquifer for cooling, using the insulated parking garage for thermal storage, orienting the building for best solar gain and carefully sizing mechanical and electrical syst-ems. In addition, we specified materials with low embodied energy and obtained them locally to minimize transportation and support the area economy. We avoided using ozone-depleting CFCs and HCFCs, and took steps to ensure the construction process itself would be environmentally friendly. Further, the compact, earth-friendly design promised to help the town meet its aim of infilling the downtown to avoid urban sprawl.

"The building is very effective for the way people use it. It's accessible to the public, and the various departments can function together because of the way it was designed. Tied in with Vivian's initiatives through lighting and air movement, those make it remarkable for what was intended to be: a spec level office building." ~Jeremy Sturgess

Further, the compact, earth friendly design promised to help the town meet its aim of infilling the downtown to avoid urban sprawl. Intent on creating a comfortable, creative work environment, we specified thermally efficient windows that open to let in the mountain air and maximize natural day lighting, used indirect lighting to reduce eyestrain and located offices on the north side to minimize solar glare. Finally, we made sure the design was flexible enough to be reused as retail or residential space (rather than demolished) if the town ever decided to move out. While many of those aspects (particularly those related to occupant comfort and building longevity) go beyond what's traditionally been incorporated into energy efficient buildings, they are key to sustainability in the sense that we were coming to understand it.

Shafraaz Kaba came aboard as we mulled the options, just in time to watch our metamorphosis begin. "I remember seeing all the C-2000 presentation boards for Banff, and hearing all those ideas being talked about," he says. "But it wasn't completely permeated throughout the office. Now there's encouragement for everyone to get up to speed and to look at all those processes in an integrative way."

Changing parameters.

Excitement mounted as we envisioned what this high-performance building could mean, both for those working inside and for the town as a whole. Superior comfort. Lifecycle energy savings. Reduced waste. Innovative, just-enough mechanical systems. Headache reducing lighting. Non-toxic finishes. Integrated landscaping. Respect as an environmental leader.

Then came the bad news: don't expect funding from C-2000. Like other owners who'd enrolled in the C-2000 program, Banff Town Council was relying on federal top-up to pay for high-performance features, and with good reason. Pilot projects such as the Crestwood designed by Teresa Coady had received $300,000 and more through the program. But two events occurred. First, federal belt-tightening struck the C-2000 program; second, those at the helm discovered that high-performance buildings, when designed as integrated units, need not cost more than their less-sustainable cousins. From the federal perspective, it made sense to delete supplemental funding. But because we didn't yet have the sophistication to fully integrate our sustainable ideas, we'd added more than we subtracted. As a result, our high performance building was going to cost more than Banff's revised budget would allow.

"When the funding was cancelled, the town came to us and said, 'Give us an ordinary building,'" Heslop recalls. "But by then we were committed to making this work. So I spent a month on the telephone, daily talking to the other partners, persuading them to carry on and finish the design for a much more advanced building." Beating the norm became even tougher as engineering and construction bids came in—all above budget.

Again integrated thinking proved invaluable, enabling us to knock costs back by more than a quarter while losing just seven percent from the building's performance. "We looked at every single choice that had been made," Heslop recalls, "and asked, 'If we alter this, will somebody's use and enjoyment of the building be impaired and will the building notice the change?' We insisted that by knocking a third off the cost, we would not cut a third from performance."

Engineer Tony Grice concurs. "We held onto the basic integrity of the building. Fortunately, the fundamentals of the strategies were so deeply imbedded that they had to stay." The cutbacks caused some fallout, however. "We reduced the lighting in the circulation spaces, and then the Sturgess team was kind enough to paint all the walls dark purple," Grice recalls, laughing. Worse, the building's performance dropped just below the fifty percent improvement mark. Still an amazing accomplishment, given the circumstances. But no longer a C-2000.

Despite its frustrations, the Banff experience crystallized for us the importance of shooting high. By initially setting the bar at the C-2000 level, Banff leaders inadvertently taught us integration, the central prerequisite for attaining sustainable design. "The fact that we had to improve the building so dramatically made us understand that no one aspect alone could provide it, which changed the way we talk about and think about design as a work process," Heslop muses. "It encouraged us to be a lot more interactive, opening up the aims and objectives to everybody. Because those goals are unachievable except together."

"C-2000 really led the charge in terms of how far could you push the design. CBIP is all about not being too radical. It's more a true market transformation program, with multiple hundreds of buildings coming through. But C-2000 continues to be a great demonstration program. Showing that you can do fifty percent makes people aspire to twenty five percent more confidently." ~Kevin Hyde

As we realized our ealier experiences in the north, now tapped an approach to listening exactly suited to affordable sustainability. We learned to integrate clients into our design team through a series of workshops that stepped from vision setting and site planning right through to the nitty gritty of personal space needs, inviting everyone who'd use the space to paint a vision of what it should be and do. To make sure that input reached the people who could address specific concerns, we'd begun pulling consulting engineers into the conversations. So it was a natural progression for us to involve an even larger circle of expertise from an even earlier point in the process.

The remoteness of the north also taught us that modest materials and simple means can achieve interesting buildings. Everything there is expensive and difficult to transport and build, not to mention costly to operate. Simplicity became a merit—and as we were now learning in Banff, that's exactly what affordable sustainability requires.

Kickstart at Keen Engineering: One building ignites a journey

Keen Engineering's work on the C.K. Choi Building for the Institute of Asian Research turned now-president Kevin Hyde into a self-proclaimed sustainable advocate. Located in Vancouver, the building boasts natural ventilation, composting toilets, low water consumption fixtures and a system that sends gray water to a subsurface wetland rather than into sewer lines.

"That's when our journey started, ten years ago. Then it was only one job; now it's half of our work," Hyde says. "My challenge has really been to transform the company, and it's pretty rewarding to see the results, it's really easy for the young people, because they come equipped with an environmental conscience. But our senior practitioners come from times when resources were infinite and impacts were negligible, or so we thought. And they're doing so much work. Converting them is the real mission."

It's instructive to note that the Keen journey has not been linear, but accelerated in recent years, as the number of champions on staff reached a critical mass. "It also occurred when we started to work more consistently with people like Vivian," Hyde says. "We just decided to work on projects we can make a difference on. My predecessor was fond of saying Keen can either make money or win awards. I've been saying that's not good enough. We've got to make money and win awards. We can do excellent work and be a good business as well."

Besides kick-starting what has since become a new business unit called "Keen Green," the C.K. Choi building earned both the 1996 Consulting Engineers Award of Merit and the 1996 BC Hydro Power Smart Award. "These benchmark buildings become like fables," Hyde observes, "and then people become attracted to you by the stories."

"We started off thinking hotshot technologies were necessary to get high performance

buildings. But when we drew up the criteria for those buildings, I threw in some

motherhood stuff about process in the last feverish moment, before it went out the

door in the fall of 1993. Then we launched a few projects and we found that, yes,

"Everybody was absolutely determined

they were reaching our performance targets, which were very tough (fifty percent

to have open windows. Sure, you could

improvement in energy alone), using technologies that were good but not super. I

make lots of arguments for sealed

talked to some of these designers, and they said, 'Of course we don't want to go out on

buildings but we had been in a building

a limb and stamp drawings where we have specified a leading-edge lighting system

where people couldn't open their

that may turn out to be a dud. If we put our stamp on it, then we're responsible, and if

windows, and we didn't want that.

there's damage, our insurance rates go up, so we tend to be conservative in specifying

Especially here, for heaven's sake where

systems. But we think it was your process requirements that turned the trick.' That

the air is so wonderful" ~Leslie Taylor

really intrigued us, because it was unexpected. So we paid more attention to it, and in

fact when the next budget cut came, we found we could still operate very successfully

with a very limited budget as long as we focused on providing support at the very

beginning stage. We gave this the name Integrated Design Process. And, like any

newish idea, it's popping up in various places." *~Nils Larsson*

Vision, Goals and Strategies

An evolving kit of client and contractor

Project Structure and Parameters

workshops coupled with close

Site Masterplan

interaction throughout the entire

Programmatic Needs

design and construction process ...

Conceptual Design

Space Planning

Building Systems Integration

Sustainable Design

Detailed Space Planning

Detailed Research and Design

Energy Modelling

Construction Partnering

Project Leadership

Quality Assurance

Post-Construction

Sustainable Deconstruction

Building technics.

Similarly, the north's bone-chilling cold prodded us to perfect a crucial element in sustainable design: the building envelope, that barrier between external elements and the indoors. In the extreme north, our worries included not only holding icy winds at bay, but keeping the site from melting out from under us.

"The time I spent with Kirby Garden, even more than my work in the north, informed how I think about building envelopes. Our northern design was an early application of those principles. And it works in any extreme climate, whether cold or wet."

Fortunately, I'd been mentored early in my career by Kirby Garden, whose status as the original building envelope guru dates back to the '60s. As a young Architect, I shadowed Garden, by then internationally known, as he parachuted in from Calgary to diagnose leakage woes on many public buildings. Like a doctor performing house calls, Garden would open his ever-present black briefcase, extract smoke pencils and diagnostic tools and give me the best possible education in how not to put a building together. I can still remember sitting on the living room floor twenty five years ago with this man, as animated as a kid in a candy store as he analyzed the blueprints spread around us.

"The roof has two components. The ceiling over the second floor is load bearing to provide for future third floor office development. On this flat decking is a torch applied MBM air seal membrane, loose laid thermal insulation and a loose laid EPDM roof membrane mechanically attached at its edges. Above this is a wood panel sheathed wood truss sloped roof with heavy grade asphalt shingles and an ice and water membrane at eaves and valleys. This creates a residential type cold attic space over the second floor, minimizing the volume of air to be conditioned in the building below."
~C-2000 Project Design Brief, 1994

Here was an expert whose fabulous bag of tricks still informs architecture today. From him I learned that an extreme-climate envelope needs two things to be sustainable: a continuous air vapor barrier that wraps the entire building and a rainscreen—a permeable outside skin with a cavity behind that's correctly pressurized to drain any moisture that soaks through. If you've ever wondered where the insulation goes on a building—"Just think about it," said Garden, "Do you swallow your coat or put it on?" What's more, we could build on that knowledge amid the north's sky-high power rates, where superior building envelopes quickly pay for themselves in energy savings.

"It was building the health centre at Grise Fiord, when we were making sure the permafrost didn't melt, that first made me conscious of the fact that we had to worry about the skin of a building." *~Richard Isaac*

Despite budget cuts in the Banff Town Hall project, we kept our eyes fixed on original targets, and met many of them. We planned to reduce water consumption by forty percent, construction waste by fifty percent, operational waste by fifty percent. Careful consideration of air changes, ventilation rates and air quality allowed us to reduce levels of CO_2, formaldehyde, volatile organic compounds, sulphur dioxide and other toxins. Operational cost savings exceeded the predicted $10 000 a year, due in part to rising energy costs.

**"The principal energy and material optimizing design strategies of the mechanical systems are: • Reduction of storm water discharge to municipal systems by diversion of storm collected from the roof and plaza to irrigate trees on the site and future park to the north. • reduction of sanitary waste water discharge to municipal systems by use of low flow fixtures and control devices. • reduction of mechanical ventilation by provision of natural ventilation to all perimeter spaces. • reduction of electrical energy consumption through the minimum use of fan and pump motors, use of high-efficiency motors on all equipment and use of variable speed drives wherever possible. • reduction of discharge of waste heat from mechanical systems through the use of air-to-air and water-to-water heat exchangers to pre-heat incoming air and water. • reduction of purchased energy consumption for heating and cooling space through use of a geo-thermal energy source." *~C-2000 Project Design Brief, 1994*

The further we went towards defining sustainable design strategies the clearer the impact became. Architecture, the way we design, the sites we select, our buildings and systems, the decisions we make daily—those are the decisions that require a clear and articulated environmental overlay.

Evolving principles as used in Banff

In committing to sustainable building design, we began to understand the environmental impact of architecture and the task implied in the word sustainable: "to keep in existence, prolong, maintain." When combined with the word design, that concept, sustainable, overlays a dimension of time and future implications on the making of a building. As architects of sustainable design, then, we do not view architecture as disposable, something that can be thrown away. Rather, we do our best to build, keep, maintain and nurture environments through time, treasuring their material, cultural and emotional value. In fact, we believe all humans share that responsibility. Our experience demonstrates that sustainable design, when integrated into every decision rather than added on, can be achieved within normal construction budgets. Furthermore, sustainable buildings reap lifetime rewards through reduced operating costs and improved workplace productivity.

- **Integrated design:**
  Exceed owner's requirements through the synergy of a team that includes architects, designers, engineers and builders as well as the client.
- **Reduce the footprint:**
  Protect the site ecosystem; reduce construction and operation wastes; minimize greenhouse gas emissions; reduce secondary environmental loading such as vehicle emissions.
- **Healthy buildings:**
  Maximize the quality of indoor air, lighting, daylighting, acoustics; provide strategies for occupants to control their environment.
- **Durable buildings:**
  Ensure each building is appropriate for intended use, yet flexible enough to accommodate future uses; demand durability and sensitive selection of materials and systems.
- **Low energy buildings:**
  Reduce energy use and cost by fifty percent.
- **Life cycle thinking:**
  Base design decisions on long- as well as short-term cost/benefit scenarios, using best available data and computing power. Commission the building to ensure it performs as expected, and that it is being operated at maximum potential.

C-2000 births: the Integrated Design Process Unexpected Offspring

The C-2000 Program for Advanced Commercial Buildings, launched in 1993 by Natural Resources Canada's CANMET Energy Technology Centre, spurred belated attention to sustainability in this country. Buildings chosen for the program must be designed to consume less than half the benchmark energy standard. In addition, they must promise minimal environmental impact, excellent indoor environment, adaptability, long-lasting components and ease of maintenance.

In the program's first two years, six proposed buildings met or exceeded the energy target, based on simulations using software designed by the U.S. Department of Energy (DOE2.1E). Unfortunately, as program manager Nils Larsson recalls, the designs were "impeccably timed" to coincide with a recession. As a result, only two were built: Green on the Grand in Kitchener Ontario and Crestwood 8 in Richmond, B.C. To the surprise of Larsson and his crew, participants used relatively conventional technologies and spent little more than the norm. Instead, they succeeded through integrated teamwork, beginning early in the design process.

Realizing that sustainable architecture could be achieved at near-normal construction cost but required more work at the design stage, C-2000 began concentrating its limited budget on design facilitation while dropping capital funding and shifting the energy benchmark from ASHRAE 90.1 to the less stringent Model National Energy Code for Buildings (MNECB).

In 1998, C-2000 began linking its efforts with a newly launched Commercial Building Incentive Program (CBIP), which attempts to penetrate a broader market by offering design funds to teams that reach the easier energy target of twenty five percent better than the benchmark MNECB. Projects supported by C-2000 expertise and CBIP dollars include the Yukon Energy Corporation head office in Whitehorse. Capital costs continue to be affordable, Larsson says, ranging from ten percent more to eleven percent less than the norm.

It's about time.

But as our experience in Banff illustrates, shrinking the payback period is not enough for the typical client. Even owners who intellectually understand the value of lifecycle costing rarely expect to reap the benefits of savings later in a building's life. In the public sector, politicians revolve; in the private sector, buildings are pawns in the real estate game. To succeed in this economic environment, the sustainable agenda must create buildings whose up-front construction costs are comparable to the norm.

Given that reality, merely adding layers of new technology is doomed to cost too much, and deliver too little. Needed are the combined smarts of experts able and willing to look at building and buildings—verb and noun—in a uniquely holistic way. Only then will we take full advantage of "solution multipliers," those magic innovations that simultaneously address energy and greenhouse emissions and cost and livability and longevity and excellence and more. In short, the whole-systems thinking prompted by integrated design offers the best solution we have for creating superior, sustainable buildings at less than exorbitant costs.

When I share my vision for integrated and sustainable design with people who don't spend their days building buildings, I can almost hear the brains ticking: "It all seems so logical, so common-sense. Why isn't that the norm?"

Fair question. And predictably, economics play a leading role in the answer. In our profession, as in so many, the 20th century saw increasing specialization, with each expert rewarded for the size of his (or sometimes her) contribution. A mechanical engineer such as Chris Jepson, for example, typically receives a percentage of the overall mechanical budget prescribed for a building. So as Jepson readily admits, "As engineers, we earn very good benefit by making the systems more complicated."

Back in the '60s, energy was cheap, so building owners worried little about what those complicated systems might consume. Then came the '70s, the energy crisis—and the drive to cut energy costs. The result? Tightly sealed buildings with shrunken windows and fewer air changes. Sick buildings, as all too many occupants soon discovered. Energy efficient to a point, yes, but horrid places to work and learn.

"Ten years ago, we started looking at sustainable designed buildings, and all of a sudden they were better. They were operating at lower energy, the people occupying them were more comfortable. We made mistakes along the way, but it was an opportunity to think out of the box, to do something a little bit different, to do something creative, at the same time giving back to environment, not always consuming. It's a reality of doing buildings in a progressive way: they kept getting better, clients kept getting happier. It's still a learning process, but the exciting thing about it is that every building is unique and different, and I'm learning so much more from the design and construction process than I did before. I want to make a living, but if I can make a living and at the same time give something back, do something unique and different that actually helps society as a whole, rather than just engineered sealed boxes that everybody's been doing for past fifty years, that's where the passion comes."
~Tony Grice

"While environmental and economic sustainability is the goal, sustainable design is the means by which we as designers have to contribute to that goal. Sustainable Design moves away from extractive and disposable systems that are energy intensive, resource inefficient and toxic towards cyclical, closed-loop systems that are restorative, dynamic and flexible."
~*HOK Guidebook to Sustainable Design*

By the '90s, it was back to the drawing board. The leading edge in Europe was already miles ahead, achieving energy savings and indoor air quality far beyond our norm. Pushed by higher energy prices and aided by triple the capital budgets, mind you, but fueled by legislation and creativity as well. Here in Canada, it wasn't until the federal C-2000 program launched in 1993 that we began to play catch-up by piloting buildings that perform "high" on multiple fronts.

It's instructive that the best of those pilots succeeded not by incorporating next-generation systems but through the synergy of fully integrated design teams. That evidence is pointing us back, in a way. Back to the neighbourhood barn raising—with a twist. Not only are our choices more complex today, but we have the expertise and technology to predict their combined impact even before a building is born. Computer Assisted Design and modelling enables us to prove that opening windows can enhance rather than detract from energy efficiency while boosting indoor air quality; that mechanical and lighting systems must be chosen in concert, because they have an impact on each other.

"The sustainability agenda goes way beyond energy. It goes to quality of the environment. Which is a core architectural issue, and always has been."

We've seen enough of these buildings in action now to know that the predictions, when carefully done with accurate data, simulate reality more accurately by the year. Convinced that sustainable architecture is far more important than any one project, and that it depends on smart choices at every level, we've taken multiple steps since Banff to equip ourselves for the journey. We "greened our specs," setting new standards for ourselves and anyone working with us by specifying sustainable solutions and materials for everything from carpet glue that doesn't off-gas toxic chemicals to support beams that contain the lowest possible embodied energy. We developed design principles and posted them publicly, both to keep ourselves honest and to invite dialogue. We began making a point of seeking partners and clients who want to walk this road with us.

Neither are we shy about spreading this gospel. We've teamed with Keen Engineering and EPCOR, for example, to launch the annual Sustainable Building Symposium, first in Edmonton and now in Calgary as well. Besides gaining the satisfaction of working with like-minded clients, we're filling the role that I've come to believe is ours as professionals with a hand in shaping our landscape, particularly in a province that's fast erecting new agora. If we don't lead the way in expanding the conversation and creating a marketplace that fits our northern landscape, who will?

"Wisdom is evolved only by synergy which is the behavior of whole aggregates not predicted by the separate behavior of character of any integral part." *~Buckminster Fuller*

Meanwhile, the stakes are rising. As the 21st century dawned, energy spiked again amid deregulation attempts and global terrorism. Terms such as "global warming" and "stewardship" moved from radical fringe to mainstream parlance, signaling an overdue shift in understanding that cannot be ignored. Media reports of people falling ill from toxic mould raise concern about the potential effects of sick buildings. Amid increasing reliance on knowledge workers and other indoor occupations, a growing chorus of complaints fuels the realization that occupant comfort correlates directly with productivity, and thus impacts the bottom line. The sustainability agenda addresses all those concerns, and none too soon.

Spreading the sustainable gospel: The sustainable building symposium.

I was really curious to see how far we could push the envelope of sustainable design. It was clear from the Banff experience that much more could be done, but also that there were many obstacles along the way. I started to think that a symposium on sustainable buildings would be an interesting way to raise the level of discussion and engage owners, designers and builders in the sharing of stories.

By this time, I had a clear sense of the importance of stories in the development of ideas. It was also becoming clear that we could start to address many of the challenges of the built environment through sustainable strategies. From indoor air quality to energy efficiency and from material selections to site orientation, architects make an enormous number of choices that affect the environment. We had to learn to make those choices more consciously, both within our own office and design team and with our clients. The stories of sustainable buildings would be the framework, going forward, for the change in attitude that we could see emerging.

I spoke to Tony Grice and Chris Jepson, both now with Keen Engineering's Green Team. They'd worked with us on the design of the Banff project, and supported the idea of a symposium. Then I talked to Cairine MacDonald of EPCOR, who was quite enthused about the prospect of participating in this initiative. Once Cairine agreed and signed on with some seed funding, the Symposium was born.

It took a while to understand what we should speak on, that first year, but we struggled through and created the first Symposium on Sustainable Buildings in Edmonton in the spring of 1997. Economics was a driving theme, and still remains a key talking point. Since then, the event has built significant momentum. By the spring of 2002, it was held in Calgary as well as Edmonton — and sold out in both cities. Rocky Mountain Institute CEO Amory Lovins brought his considerable insight to a keynote evening address outlining the business sense of sustainability and UBC Professor of Architecture Ray Cole opened a full day of learning with an impassioned plea for the social as well as environmental imperatives of sustainable design. Speakers over the years have included Mayor Ross Risvold of Hinton, Bernie Kreiner, Hinton's Town Manager, Kevin Hydes of Keen Engineering and many others. Success stories and case studies abound.

Now entering its sixth year, under the determined leadership of Dagny Alston as conference coordinator, the Symposium continues to grow, speaking to building owners, school boards, college and university leadership, municipal, provincial and federal government leaders. We're teaching courses on sustainable design strategies to architects across the country, and learning as fast as we teach. A recent cross-country sustainable design course drew architects, engineers and builders to seminars from Halifax to Vancouver. Finally, we're starting to see some of these ideas becoming more mainstream. But I'm still curious. I really wonder what it will take to imbed sustainability in the mainstream strategies for many more aspects of building design and construction.

I remember, a number of years ago, giving a paper on the time lag of technology transfer at an international conference on building research. To watch the evolution of thinking, I had followed a series of health centres, designed over a period of two decades. My analysis indicated that it took 20 to 25 years from the time an idea is first published in professional journals to the time it enters common use in the construction and design industry.

Staggered, I didn't really believe this result until a much more senior colleague came up to discuss what I had found. He laughed. "Of course," he said. "Why would you imagine the time line to be any less than a full generation?"

I guess that the same will be the case with sustainable design. It will still be "new" for the next 5 to 10 years—and then it will become increasingly mainstream until, by about the year 2020, it will be fully integrated into the practice of design and construction.

We formed the Sustainable Buildings Consortium, created a planning committee and kept refining the program year after year. With the involvement of key stakeholders like Alberta's Climate Change Central, the cities of Edmonton and Calgary and others, we continue to refine the stories of sustainable design.

Hinton

Government

Centre

A bridge between.

A bridge. That's how the Hinton Government Centre functions in the foothills community of 10,000 that it serves. Midway between the once-distinct communities of Hinton and Drinnan, the building provides a connecting point between hill and valley, industry and environment, rural and urban, past and future. In many ways, that's what this project has proven for Vivian Manasc and her sustainable team: a bridge between what began in Banff and what will become the norm in future sustainable projects, a satisfying shift from aiming for C-2000 to exceeding that goal with a structure that outperforms the Model National Energy Code by a full 52 per cent. So perhaps it's no wonder that a design element particularly favoured by both town and team is the wooden bridge visitors cross to reach the three-storey building. Were this a poem, the bridge might seem almost too obvious a metaphor. But in its context, it makes powerful aesthetic sense.

Spending a day in Hinton, a community I've long known only as the final gas'n'go spot enroute to nearby Jasper National Park, I first cross the bridge to meet the town's Director of Engineering and Development, Dale Rhyason, and Development Information Officer Dwayne Breitkreutz. Dale and I had connected in a past life at the City of Edmonton, where he headed environmental efforts before retiring to spend more time near the mountains, so I figure he'll give me the straight scoop. The three of us head to a nearby buffet and cut to the chase between bites of Szechuan and rice.

It's soon clear that Dwayne's life has been a blur since January 2001, when town staff moved into their new home. As word of the centre's innovative features spreads, his role as Development Information Officer has expanded to include a distinctly new chunk called "tour guide." Behind the scenes, meanwhile, he's the one phoning the design and construction team when things don't quite run as intended, whether the culprit's as simple as a chunk of solder in the line or as hard to diagnose as the cross-wired panel that caused lights in one washroom to flick off when someone exited the washroom in the floor above.

As those left sitting in a dark washroom those first days might attest, the settling-in brought its share of puzzlement. In a building with fewer bells and whistles than the norm, solutions are often as low-tech as uncrossing those wires, yet the fact that this is an integrated structure gives a unique twist to the business of learning how to run it. "It's a good example of how much work there is after you occupy a building like this, getting up to speed and trying to fit the pieces of the puzzle together," Dale muses. But as we talk, it's equally clear this duo believes any start-up snafus are small price to pay for the promise imbedded in this $4.7-million structure.

"I've been very impressed," Dale says. "When you go into an energy efficient building, you think of something with small windows, something that's uncomfortable or not very good looking, but this building defies all of those norms. It's an attractive building, it's very comfortable inside, it's open, there's lots of window space. All of that stuff you don't expect."

Dwayne dons his tour guide hat as we wind back up to the government centre along a treelined and curbless road that would be at home in a campground—an aura that's far from accidental, as I later discover. As we explore the interior, it becomes clear that the spaces incorporate a rich blend of staff input (received through the rigorous Manasc Isaac workshop process) and team knowledge about sustainable architecture. Many assets are clearly visible, including opening windows that give staff members light, fresh air and a sense of control over their space.

"When I'm in here, my responsibility, if the building is designed this way, is to go that extra step. I want to make it perform like it was intended." *~Dwayne Breitkruitz*

From Dwayne's point of view, though, the most intriguing features are hidden within the floor, walls and bowels of the building, particularly in the building envelope. "It's as if the entire structure is wearing a super-insulated down parka", he says. "There's some heat transfer happening through our windows and walls, but no conveyance, no draft. If I were building a house today, I'd be doing this."

Dwayne's enthusiasm takes me back to a recent Sustainable Building Symposium, where Hinton Town Manager Bernie Kreiner described how staff have responded to their new home. When informally surveyed, they divided into two camps, he told symposium participants. One segment was simply content with the comfortable, low-hassle environment and happy to leave it at that; a second, and growing, contingent is "excited about what we're doing, and want to do more, taking the message of this building to a higher level."

Kreiner finds that second group particularly intriguing. "There's an interesting mindset change in how they're interacting with the space," he told his audience. A new sense of ownership has spawned interesting discussions, and those, in turn, are escalating environmental action. The town has shifted from plastic to living plants as office decor, for example, and an e-group is advancing a bevy of sustainable operating ideas. Besides being "very user friendly," the town manager concluded, sustainable buildings "change how we behave."

But Hinton, Alberta, Canada, population 10,000, stands 270 km. west of Edmonton and 80 km. east of the Jasper National Park townsite. Established in 1958, Hinton is a resource-rich town, home to forestry and a pulp mill since the '50s and modern coal mines in the '70s and '80s. The pulp mill, now significantly modernized, stands between what began as two communities, Hinton and Drinnan, known to residents as the Hill and the Valley.

"I realize my perception of Hinton has been forever changed. Whenever I zip down the Yellowhead route to Jasper these days, I look up to the southwest just as the Switzer Drive underpass nears, to salute the Hinton Government Centre glinting through the trees. If I were building today, you can bet I'd be borrowing a few ideas, too." ~Cheryl Mahaffy

"For me, this office is like being out in the bush. Some of us missed our old offices at first, with the cars going by on the highway.   But I look out there and I see squirrels, and I see the mountains; it's wonderful", says a first floor tenant from the Province of Alberta's Children's Servises.

Building the bridge.

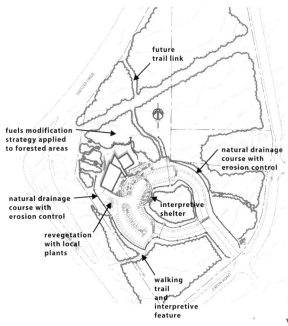

future
trail link

fuels modification
strategy applied
to forested areas

natural drainage
course with
erosion control

natural drainage
course with
erosion control

interpretive
shelter

revegetation
with local
plants

walking
trail
and
interpretive
feature

Vivian: My first hint that Hinton might be looking for a bridge —and a building to go with it—came at a late 1998 conference hosted by Edmonton Mayor Bill Smith. "Meet the North," it was called, but in our case it turned out to be Meet the West. Having just discovered that Hinton had lost much of its town hall to a November fire, I met then-Mayor Ross Risvold in one of those fortuitous staircase connections, and commiserated with him about the loss. In Edmonton to speak from his considerable experience in fostering sustainable communities, Risvold soon realized we shared a wavelength and invited our team to make a point of connecting with his.

The town put out a call for architects, specifically seeking sustainably inclined firms who'd done award-winning work in wood. Fortunately, several of our previous projects appear among Canadian Wood Council case studies, reflecting our affinity for wood as a renewable resource with low embodied energy and high aesthetic value.

It wasn't long before a trio of us headed toward the Rocky Mountains to Hinton, where we were selected to assist Council in making a critical decision. Still at the very early stages of figuring out how to replace its burned headquarters, the town needed to hear from citizens; between us, Architect Derek Heslop, Landscape Architect Bob Gibbs and I led 30 focus groups before leaving town.

"The history of Hinton was of a place in two parts. The people of the town were looking for a place to share in common." *~Derek Heslop*

It became clear that Hinton's options ranged widely, from rebuilding at the burned site to renovating other space to starting afresh on a new site. Although renting elsewhere looked cheapest from a short-term perspective, Mayor Risvold and his community understood the wisdom of factoring in sustainability. On those terms, a new, energy-efficient building made imminent sense, saving as much as $30,000 a year in energy costs, not to mention the promise of improved comfort and productivity. Town leaders also appreciated the symbolic value of stewarding resources and showcasing wood in a community whose livelihood depended on coal for decades and remains closely tied to surrounding forests.

"We're leading edge without being bleeding edge," says then mayor Ross Risvold, who caught sight of sustainability's potential while serving on external networks such as Climate Change Alberta, the Foothills Model Forest and the Federation of Canadian Municipalities. After much debate and pondering, council voted unanimously for a new, sustainable, wood-based structure on town land located midway between the two historic communities that combined to form Hinton.

"I'm always amazed how much wood is trucked back and forth between Alberta and British Columbia alone. It makes a lot of sense to also think of transportation as a part of sustainable building."
~Bernie Kreiner

When council's plans hit the coffee shops, fire of another sort broke out. The new construction would leave holes in the rental market, some said; how could the town ignore its policy of not competing with private building owners? Instead, why not purchase its interim office on the appropriately named Government Street, which after all stood on land originally reserved for municipal use? By the time the project's borrowing bylaw came up for third reading, concerned citizens had easily gathered the 10 per cent of voter signatures required to demand a plebiscite.

As debate swirled the streets, councillors remained convinced of the project's benefits, defying stereotypes that assume a town fed by forestry, oil and coal would care little for conservation. Having set the wheels in motion for a legacy head-quarters, environmentally sustainable as well as technologically advanced, the Town intended to stay the course. It helped that financing was falling into place, aided by a provincial decision to rent significant space in a new building.

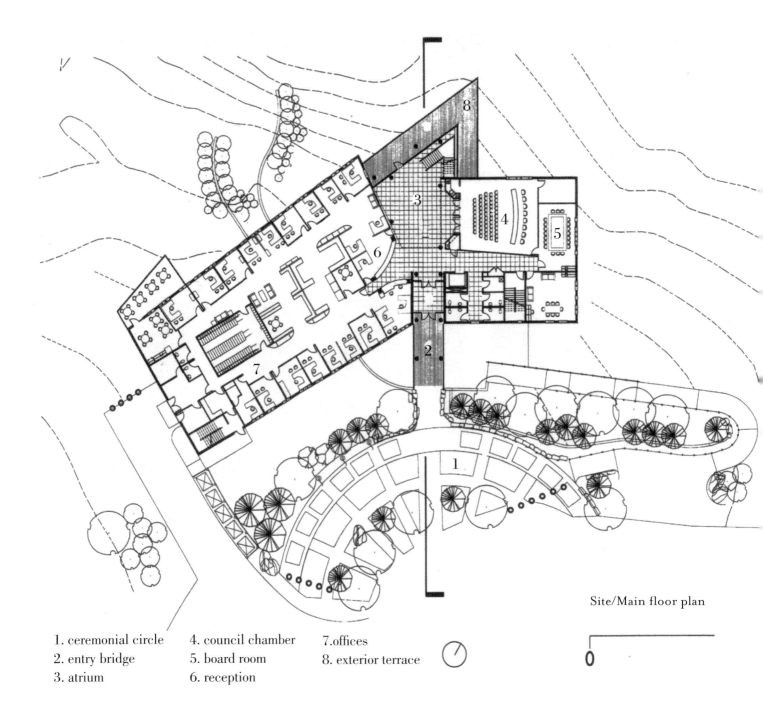

Site/Main floor plan

1. ceremonial circle
2. entry bridge
3. atrium
4. council chamber
5. board room
6. reception
7. offices
8. exterior terrace

0

In the end, 67 per cent of Hinton voters endorsed council's vision. The six-month hiatus caused by the plebiscite delayed move-in until January 2001, forcing staff to make do in a former hardware store an extra half year. On the plus side, the thorough airing of views prompted greater understanding as the project proceeded.

"Always design a thing by considering it in its next context—a chair in a room, a room in a house, a house in an environment, and environment in a city plan." *~Eliel Saarinen*

Living with the land.

The Hinton Government Centre proved an exciting sustainable design challenge in part because its wooded and sloping 6.5-hectare (16.2-acre) site offered an opportunity to build in harmony with existing terrain rather than bulldozing it flat. Landscape Architect Stefan Johanson worked with us to make that happen.

"The overriding premise was to keep the natural feel of the surrounding area and minimize impacts to trees and wildlife habitat," Johanson says. That desire, coupled with the fact that nearby storm sewers were already close to capacity, prompted the team to let runoff percolate into the soil rather than piping it away. "And I threw in the idea of a roadway based loosely on campgrounds and parkways, with trees closer to the road," Johanson recalls. The resulting curbless, canopied approach incorporates serpentine bends that deftly circumvent drainage routes. "So as you go into the site, you don't know what's around the corner, and there's an element of surprise. And then when you actually arrive, a sense of awe."

Emerging from a dense thicket of conifers, visitors enter a circular drive surrounding a public gathering spot. "We created a ceremonial circle loosely based on the First Nations in the region, who had seasonal gathering points and hunting camps," Johanson explains. That sense of history is further amplified by footsteps in the circle, and by interpretive signs describing the many who have crossed Hinton land—hunters, trappers, coal miners and foresters, to name a few.

Hinton is a place where forest meets urban life. There's beauty in that, but also inherent danger of fire. Rather than avoiding wood as a building material or stripping the trees back from the building, as past practice might dictate, the team worked with Alberta Forest Service to create a prototype wildland-urban interface. "Using the government centre as ground zero, we created concentric circles of firebreaks," Johanson explains. Particularly near the building, the forest was thinned and stripped of any dead wood that might serve as fuel, reducing a fire's ability to step up into the trees, shoot to the top, catch the wind and mushroom.

"This small cluster of trees is very valued in our community. So it makes sense that we have not chosen a manicured solution to landscaping. And it will be low maintenance." ~*Bernie Kreiner*

Some beautiful old spruce and lesser species needed to come down, but even those became part of an overall effort to use local materials wherever possible, increasing the site's rootedness while reducing transportation costs. "Any trees we felled were taken to the mill and we did a swap, exchanging our timber for dry timber," Johnson explains. "In essence, timbers on site were retained." Dozens of those large peeled beams became signature aspects of the building, inside and out; others were turned into flagpoles, site furniture and mulch. Similarly, limestone and boulders found onsite or donated by local mines serve as groundcover, retaining walls, amphitheatre and impromptu seating during civic events.

"One of our most important initiatives was the use of live soils," Johanson adds. The top layer of humus was stockpiled during road and site excavation, seeds intact, and carefully reintroduced when construction was complete so seeds could sprout. "Even though you may be unfamiliar with Hinton, those native plants give you just a clue of the place."

Recycled plastics also find a home in this natural looking environment, providing a web of support along fire access routes. "It looks like grass and sidewalk, but underneath we've put plastic pavers, a sort of geotechnical web, so heavy equipment can drive on it," Johanson explains.

Minimizing construction impact and waste remained a key goal throughout the project, he adds. "The contractor had to be very careful about taking down forest cover. Try doing that with a bulldozer." For those not driven by shared ethic, a construction document set the tone, stipulating reuse and recycling and demanding durable, earth-friendly materials. On-site supervision helped hold crews to the standard.

Johanson discovered that, with extra attention in the planning phase, sustainable landscaping proves remarkably affordable. "You need to do a little more site analysis. But in the end, this type of design is equivalent in capital costs if not even less," he says. In fact, natural drainage that avoids curbs, gutters and underground piping offers municipalities an intriguing antidote to ballooning budgets and at-capacity sewer systems. "It's just a matter of setting a watermark. It's amazing how many people see the site and say, 'What a great idea! How come we didn't think of this?'"

Like others in our team, Johanson views the Hinton project as a personal watermark, a standard-setter. "This approach is now my first course of action, my default position," he says. "I've realized that if you do something else, it lessens your design."

A sustainable signature.

Set against its forest backdrop, the 3,000-square-metre government centre pulls visitors across the signature bridge, into a spacious atrium sunlit by a two-storey prow of windows. To the left stands a reception counter for the town offices, whose staff enjoy window seats along the perimeter of the west wing. At right is a corridor leading to meeting and work rooms for the mayor and six town councillors. A double door leads into Council Chambers; beyond, a wide wooden stair invites traffic to the top floor, rented by the Province of Alberta for Sustainable Development staff. Below, the walk-out lower floor holds provincial offices for Children's Services and the Alberta Alcohol and Drug Abuse Commission.

With its view of forests and the Athabasca River Valley, its huge wooden timbers and its stately stairs, the atrium has quickly gained favour as a ceremonial spot. Some ask why this signature

"We don't have a green, manicured lawn. It's different, because most government centres would have a massive groomed area. But it does illustrate that sustainability—all the little things that accumulate to reduce the environmental footprint." ~Ross Risvold

space isn't angled more directly to face Hinton's signature view—the distant Rocky Mountains. But it's all the result of careful solar analysis that pointed the massive expanse of glass toward the north, where it can absorb and vent warm air without overheating. Rotating the building 7% provided an increase in modelled energy savings from 43% to 52% below the model national energy rate. The building as a whole is shaped and oriented to provide the best possible compromise between the long south/north line that would let in the most daylight and the compact shape that reduces the exterior exposure to temperature extremes and wind. Even the way the roof sweeps up over the office areas is calculated to carry strong prevailing winds away from the south face of the building and shelter the public entry.

As the design progressed, our team combined expanding knowledge about sustainable architecture with input received through workshops and visits to other projects that might serve as models, and staff who came along voted for wide working corridors rather than dark and narrow hallways. And everybody wanted windows.

"Vivian and Richard are sort of harbingers of the way people are starting to accept and appreciate how landscaping can fit within the sustainable agenda. They're on the edge of where we're going, and they pick a lot of the same consultants for these projects, so we're aware of each other and we try to complement each other. I appreciate the creativity, the cost savings, the environmental spin and of course I like to work with good people. It has got me hooked. Now I'm basically preaching this in all my projects." ~*Stefan Johanson*

Because the team paid heed to that input, the building is functional, a crucial if sometimes undersold aspect of sustainable design. Those most apt to serve walk-in citizens, such as billing and planning staff, sit nearest the entrance with a small conference room nearby for conversations that require privacy. The sun-filled offices surround a large central area for shared office gear. The storage vault eats up less space than in previous quarters, thanks to ceiling-height filing cabinets on tracks that can be rolled up against each other.

Lighting throughout the building follows the sustainable maxim of high solar, low glare. Raised ceilings coupled with high windows in exterior offices allow natural light into the central shared space. Wherever possible, those windows open to allow fresh air in as well. High-efficiency lighting units bounce more than 90 per cent of the beam off the ceiling, creating a soft glow that reduces eyestrain. Motion sensors and automatic controls ensure lights are used only when someone's in the room.

Thanks to the building's high performance envelope, the high-efficiency furnace is significantly smaller than the norm. And an ingenious system draws cooling power from the municipal water supply, eliminating the need for an air conditioner. For the people of Hinton, it's a particular point of pride that their headquarters has left energy-gobbling coolants and compressors behind.

As in Banff, and like most C-2000 teams, we chose minimalist or passive strategies rather than high-tech bells and whistles, reducing mechanical and electrical needs through synergy between the building, its users and its environment. Our use of wood provides an excellent case in point. Besides all the usual reasons for choosing wood—low embodied energy, affordability, durability, speed of delivery, flexibility of design—it's a material that made perfect sense in a community whose heritage breathes forests and forestry, where local supplies and skills are abundant.
In fact, the building contains four generations of Alberta-grown wood materials: 50-foot columns as major roof supports, dimensional wood studs and plates for perimeter wall framing, glulam beams for floor and roof supports and engineered wood joists and sheathing for framing.

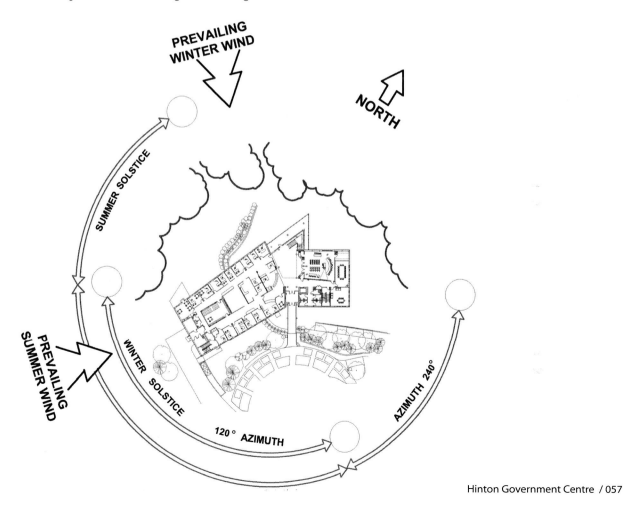

"I think the government centre has been a very, very positive venture. It has shown you can do this kind of thing, and now these concepts are being duplicated. Hinton has got a tremendous amount of recognition, as has Vivian's group. Some of our trades people weren't aware of the things you can do, so we're also building capacity within the community. You need these demonstration projects. We're just happy we could be involved." ~*Ross Risvold*

"You've got to involve everyone, from start to finish. That's easy to say, but hard to do."

~Bernie Kreiner

"If you can light a building using natural

"In Alberta, we're blessed most of the year to have

lighting, there are incredible energy

natural light, and we wanted to take advantage of that.

benefits but even more incredible human

We believe in outside air, not closed air-conditioned

benefits. The most successful lighting

boxes, so we wanted to open this building up."

system is the one you don't notice."

~*Bernie Kreiner*

~Tony Grice

Selected sustainable building strategies: Hinton Government Centre

Site conservation:

Access and parking located to maximize site preservation. Topsoil and native seed materials stockpiled and re-used. Runoff from roads and parking managed on-site rather than through storm sewers.

Building form and orientation:

Situated to reduce heat and glare from prevailing winds and low summer sun, yet slightly bent to maximize mountain views. Native and supplemental vegetation provide natural shelter.

Daylighting:

Reduced need for artificial light by keeping the building quite narrow, using large windows and locating functional spaces for best exposure. High efficiency indirect lighting augmented by occupancy and daylight sensors.

Windows:

Opening windows provide local ventilation, improve comfort and reduce cooling costs. High performance windows with spectrally selective glazing are tightly sealed to a superior building envelope.

Heating & ventilation:

Four-pipe fan coil systems with high efficiency heating and cooling units, sized to take advantage of superior insulation. Cooling provided by closed—loop Municipal water supply. Underfloor (access-floor) air distribution system in town offices optimizes comfort, flexibility and efficiency.

Materials:

Wood structure and cladding maximizes use of local materials and minimizes environmental impact. Trees removed selectively from the site, reused in building structure.

Waste Management:

Indoor and outdoor facilities linked to the municipal recycling system. Construction waste managed and separated on site. Landfill diversions considered by reuse and resale of selected waste.

Reduced emissions:

Achieves 52 per cent reduction in greenhouse gas emissions by cutting operational energy use in half.

Lifecycle savings:

No increased capital cost for improved building performance; annual energy cost savings exceed $30,000.

Community development:

Demonstrates leadership, augments local skills, provides the profile and confidence needed to tackle similar leading-edge projects.

Access floor.

In designing the Hinton centre, we pushed the sustainable agenda forward by proposing an access flooring system. Already used in several high-performance buildings in Vancouver and favoured by firms such as Keen Engineering, the access floor pulls the walking surface and subfloor apart so that power, electronics, ventilation and other essential systems can run between.

The access floor "turns everything upside down," notes electrical engineer Tony Grice. "Normally you put the lighting and most services in the ceiling; everything comes down from up top. But we're not worried about how hot or cold it is at the ceiling, because nobody is occupying that space. What we're concerned with is people's comfort right at the work station. Instead of trying to blow air down from the ceiling, now you can adapt the air supply so it actually is right at the desk." Because the building's highly insulated walls and windows block more heat and cold than the norm, there's no need for the usual concentration of vents around outside edges. Instead, moveable diffusers can be clustered around desks, allowing individuals to adjust the amount of ventilation to suit their varied preferences. As with the indirect lighting, which is high in quality yet low in wattage, Grice notes, "we're not trying to force air down, just trying to create a nice comfortable environment using as little energy as possible."

Besides consuming less energy, underfloor climate control improves air quality, says Chris Jepson, who designed the mechanical system. As spent air and toxins rise from such sources as laser printers, they're not forced back into people's lungs but are exhausted at such spots as the double-storey atrium. As an added benefit, warmer overall air temperatures decrease humidity and thus reduce the likelihood of mould and disease.

Because an access floor is essentially an open cavity of space topped by squares of floor covering, it's easier to reconfigure space, update wiring and change building functions. "Life is so easy when you have that floor system," says Town Manager Bernie Kreiner, noting that staff are pleased there are no longer "ladders kicking around" as repairs are made. Not that functionality has eliminated grumbles from those who can't seem to find that perfect temperature, even after numerous follow up visits from engineers to "tweak the system." Overall temperature is computer controlled, with one thermostat per multi-office zone. It might be ideal for each office to have its own thermostat, but most budgets prohibit that degree of perfection.

"Regardless of the type of building you put in, not every person is going to have the same level of comfort unless they can actually control their own space totally." *~Dale Rhyason*

"Now of course the fact is that conventional systems don't work well at all. The minute you let people have any say at all in the planning and design of their space, they tell you the heating doesn't work and the cooling doesn't work and the lighting doesn't work and the day lighting isn't adequate and the windows don't open. But nobody expects traditional systems to work well. People do expect a higher level of performance of sustainable systems, which is what we expect as well."

At the leading edge.

Wandering the ceremonial circle during the May 2001 official opening of the Hinton Government Centre, Town Manager Bernie Kreiner heard reassuring chatter. Residents were happy to see that the building is attractive while not elaborate, fitting community character through careful use of local wood, stone, glass, concrete and masonry; that it's sustainable, promising to consume one-third less energy than the old town hall while tripling the occupancy; that it stuck to budget, despite escalating construction costs as the Alberta economy boomed. "Like any change, it was difficult for some people," Kreiner muses, recalling plebiscite debates. "But the late adapters have adapted now. I'm pleasantly surprised how little an issue it is anymore."

Former Mayor Ross Risvold hears similar comments in his travels. Some who voted against borrowing for new construction will never change their mind, he says, but most take pride in calling this high-performance building theirs. In the fine tradition of prophets from afar, the attitude shift is being fueled by a series of awards and accolades, including laudatory coverage in Canadian Living, finalist status in Alberta's environmentally focused Emerald Awards and selection as Project of the Year for Structures-Facilities by the Alberta Chapter of the Canadian Public Works Association.

Indeed, the building's success has accelerated Hinton's sustainability journey. Besides an expanding array of energy retrofits, the town is tackling such leading-edge projects as solar-heating its swimming pool and drawing methane from its landfill site. Ahead lie such ideas as harnessing the wind, which blows hard this close to the mountains, and tapping unusual geothermal formations below Hinton's feet. Says Kreiner, "it's reached a point where it has become a mindset rather than a project-based approach."

"They did computer modelling to try to ensure we had maximum efficiency. So what we have is a building that looks nicer from what we would think of as the back of the site. But sustainability was the driving force, so we didn't sacrifice or back off on sustainability for physical appearance regarding how we would place the building on the land." ~Ross Risvold

Others in the community are walking that same road. Weldwood of Canada Ltd. (Hinton Division), the town's major employer, has asked us to incorporate sustainable strategies and concepts into its new administrative centre. Plans are also afoot for a 45-hectare (110-acre) Hinton eco-industrial park that will generate its own light and heat while sending runoff to a wetland rather than into storm sewers. Onsite generation works particularly well in Alberta, where energy producers can sell excess energy to the grid, but could be replicated anywhere, says former mayor Ross Risvold, who's among the project's prime advocates. "What it takes is a cultural change, a paradigm shift to a new way of thinking." The federal Green Municipal Fund is expected to join Town Council in helping to finance a feasibility study and plan, based in part on Hinton's strong track record. "Once we've moved ahead, other communities will take a closer look at it," Risvold predicts. "Very few want to be the first out of the chute."

Being among the first is changing behaviour not only in but toward the community, says Risvold, who remains plugged into sustainability networks as a consultant even though he decided against running for re-election after 12 years on Town Council. "Because of our profile as a go-to town, opportunities come up to try new technology. People say, 'take it to Hinton, because they're already there. You won't have to start at square one to educate them.'"

Equipped to choose.

For our design team, tackling a sustainable design challenge such as Hinton is not only professionally responsible, but fun. Unlike earlier attempts to correct energy excess, which became a same-old routine of shrinking windows and reducing air changes, sustainability is multifaceted. Where those earlier approaches made occupants increasingly unhappy and sick, sustainability aims to improve on the norm. Each next project challenges us to up the standard, building on what we learned in the last.

In large measure, sustainable architecture succeeds where those earlier approaches failed precisely because it takes a holistic view of the project at hand. Rather than zeroing in on energy alone, we pay attention to comfort, air quality, durability, materials, aesthetics, building systems, community context site and numerous other factors. There's power in considering all those factors simultaneously, because that's when both synergies and conflicts pop to the surface.

"One of most innovative features was using the town's water distribution system for cooling, which is relatively rare. But the conditions have to be just right. The amount of water that's flowing past the building has to be constant and at great enough volume so the heat put back into the system won't disrupt the system." *~Lorne Stadnick*

Equally important, integrated design forces us to wrestle through tough choices. In Hinton, for example, the best orientation from a solar standpoint put the building's striking atrium at the back of the site and took minimal advantage of distant mountain views. We did catch a bit of the mountain skyline by bending one wing of the building to the northwest, but chose to leave the atrium at the back for sustainability—where it still makes a strong interior statement. Budget debates also arise as we weigh the potential benefit of leading-edge technology against proven strategies that might free up dollars for superior windows or finishes.

In short, we are becoming better sustainable architects to the extent that we are learning to make skillful tradeoffs. Learning, for example, how many thermostats it takes to balance staff comfort against the budget. Learning where and when access floors make sense. Learning how much we can expect from the people who operate the buildings we design, and what must be built fail-safe. In the Hinton project, our ability to make those tradeoffs benefited from three key assets: prior experience, an expanded team and a committed client.

Prior experience: Banff gave us the real-world understanding that comes from actually putting a high performance building together and watching it run. "With the Hinton Government Centre, we started exactly where we'd left off with Banff, even to the point of taking out the old drawings," muses project architect Derek Heslop. "For a lot of reasons, we were able to look at the choices we'd made in Banff and see that they were applicable in Hinton as well." "Having come so close to C-2000 in Banff", he adds, "we had a high degree of confidence. It was not a question of 'Can we do this?' but 'How are we going to choose to do it?'"

"We've been dealing with theory. Now there's a whole validation process going on. What we're learning is that theory works even better than we thought it would." *~Tony Grice*

Expanded team: Second, we enlarged our pool of expertise, particularly by adding an energy consultant. In the years since Banff, C-2000's Nils Larsson had put us in touch with Gord Shymko, who'd migrated from the west coast to our backyard in Calgary, setting up an integrated engineering and computer modeling consultancy that provided skills we hadn't yet mastered. Now Shymko worked in sync with our design team, using software developed for the U.S. Department of Energy (DOE2.1E) to depict the Hinton building in 3-D and then simulate how differing design choices would affect performance. Beyond identifying specific places to save energy, he helped us eliminate redundancies and address glitches before they were built, thus reducing capital costs. Based on prior involvement in many of the C-2000 buildings scattered across Canada, he knew that a high performance building would operate within five per cent of his projections—and that most anomalies could be traced to operating glitches rather than design errors.

Committed client: Bolstered by the evidence, Hinton leaders took the gamble of exploring new territory with us. Some clients might find it disconcerting to realize that their building is our learning ground, and tug us back to a place that feels safer. Not Hinton. This client's commitment to sustainability was crucial to the success of this project, as was its openness to inclusive, integrated design. Having seen the results, town leaders now urge others to pay equal heed to process rather than focusing solely on product.

Vision for the Hinton Government Centre; Achieved through integrative planning; Reflects the community it serves; Responds to both site and intended function; Is energy-efficient and minimizes its impact on the environment; Uses available skills and materials that reflect the Hinton economy; Creates a positive legacy for future generations.

The notion of all-inclusive input at the option assessment and design stages was very powerful," recalls Kreiner from his seat as town manager. Not that it's like falling off a log, he adds, using an apt metaphor in a forestry town. "The more consultative you are, the more you'll come across people who are not early innovators, who are satisfied with what's currently acceptable instead of what could be. But my advice is to set aside your presumptions and go at it open-mindedly. Risk a bit, as we did with the access floor. The result may be very different from what you're used to, but it doesn't have to be less desirable."

Together, town and team crafted a structure remarkably in tune with the vision first outlined as we sat down to dream. Concretely as well as figuratively, this is a headquarters building whose location, design and materials visibly link, and link to, the community. It serves both its community and its environment while creating a positive legacy for the future. The building put the Town of Hinton exactly where it wants to be: at the forefront.

That's also where citizens expect Hinton to be, Kreiner contends. "Based on what we saw in Hinton, I believe the public is ahead of us," he says. "And that surprised me. We billed this project on cost savings. But if I were building a municipal building now, I would bill it as an e-building. Call it an environmentally sustainable building. It will sell."

Athabasca Health Facility: Pre-tender Report, July 1998

The Athabasca Health Facility if a unique community-based, multi-level health facility located adjacent to the Town of Stoney Rapids on the Black Lake Reserve, in northern Saskatchewan.

The facility is a replacement of the hospital currently serving the Athabasca Basin (located at Uranium City) and creates an opportunity to integrate the physical, mental and social health needs of the region into one efficient facility.

Design philosophy

The facility design is based on four guiding principles:
• The building must integrate and respond to its site, as well as to its functional programme.
• The building must reflect the vision of the communities it serves.
• The building must be energy-efficient and minimize its impact on the environment.
• The building must be designed so it can readily be constructed in the community with available skills and materials.

The design is premised on the outcomes of a series of consultative workshops held in each of the communities, with community members, and a second series of func-tional workshops held with staff from Uranium City, Fond du Lac and LaRonge.
The overall design of the proposed facility is based on the direction given to the design team, and includes:

• Clear circulation - direct access from a warm south-facing entry into the main spine of the facility.
• A central nursing station that can supervise the emergency entry, the main entry and in-patient areas.
• All in-patient rooms facing the river and the rapids.
• An Emergency Department that is compact and efficient.
• Adequate central space to accommodate large numbers of clinic patients and visitors.
• A building that is oriented east-west to optimize its thermal performance and to the views of the Fond du Lac River to the north.

Energy conservation strategies

Several strategies were employed in the building and site design to reduce consumption of water and energy during building operation:
• East-West building orientation reduces solar heat gain and need for cooling,
• Rectangular building plan provide compact area inside a minimum area of exterior surface wall,
• Sloped shed roof minimizes exposure of exterior walls to prevailing north-east winds,
• Design of windows and spectrally selective glazing maximizes comfortable daylight in the building interior while minimizing solar heat gain from sunlight,
• Exterior sunshade devices reduce glare and solar heat gain while increasing daylighting in interior rooms,
• High level of insulation used to retain energy generated in winter within building by heating, lights, equipment and activities and to keep out excessive solar heat gain in summer,
• A fully adhered air barrier membrane covers the entire exterior building surface under the insulation to minimize air movement through the exterior wall,
• Small and highly efficient ventilation systems are used to closely match the highly variable demand for air in different space at different times of the day and months of the year,
• Low flow plumbing fixture are used throughout the building to reduce the demand for treated water and the volume of waste water to be removed,
• Highly efficient direct/indirect lights give high quality electric light to interior spaces and balance daylight admitted by the exterior windows,

These strategies were designed to work together with one another to reduce energy use and utility cost, improve reliability and quality of system performance and to facilitate good, long term facility management and maintenance using local building operations staff and remote facility monitoring and management.

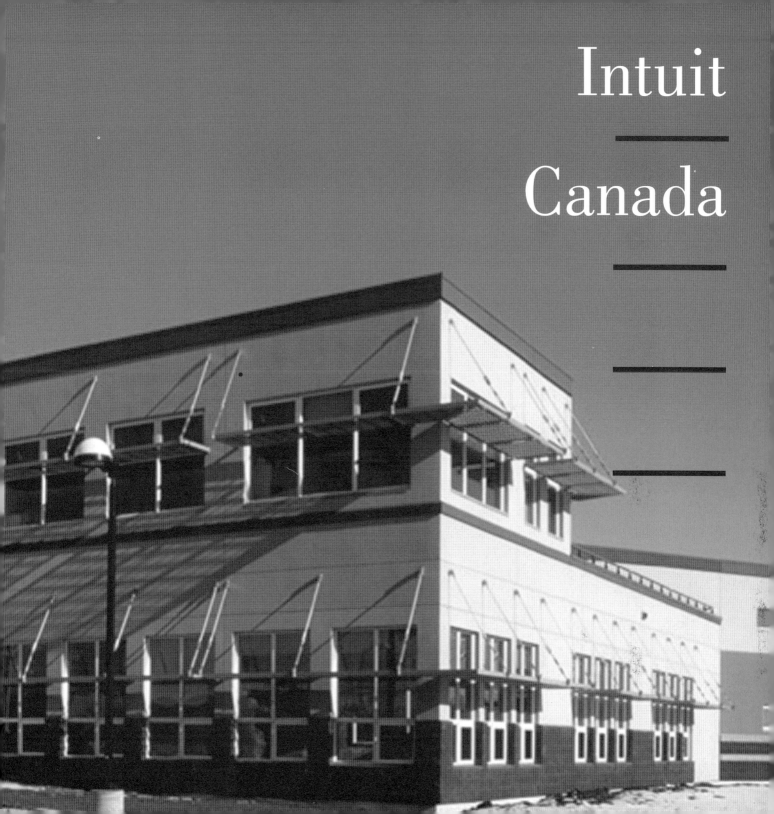

Intuit
___
Canada

Intuit's Canadian headquarters:
A place to call home.
Hyper-tracked. High-tech. High-touch. Fun.

It's May 2000, and that's my last leisurely moment in a project whose hyper-tracked schedule leaves team members stunned long after onlookers quit calling us crazy. As I discover when the call does connect, Intuit needs new headquarters—now. Within six months, to be precise; in construction, that's as good as now. The window of opportunity is very short: shoehorned into makeshift quarters, staff must move before updates to Intuit's Quicken^{TM}, QuickBooks^{TM} and QuickTax^{TM} software hit the shelves and the help desk heats up.

Beyond high-speed construction, Intuit Canada demands two things from this building: high-tech muscle, but also high-touch creature comforts. Since 1992, when Bruce Johnson and Chad Frederick cheekily launched WinTax for then-new Windows and attracted an alliance with giant U.S.-based Intuit, its expanding suite of finance software has earned a loyal following in Canada, and now Great Britain. Fully aware that its creative crew, already nearly 300 strong, deserves top credit for accelerating the enterprise into the fast lane, Johnson and Frederick insist on equipment and ambience that will nurture existing staff—and attract new talent. Given the often competitive market for high-tech workers, and given Edmonton's relative distance from many high-tech hotspots, this duo is fully aware that a negative environment could suck away the ingenuity that is Intuit's lifeblood. More than a software development site, more than a call centre, this firm needs a creativity percolator, by November.

Pretty amazing parameters. In fact, as we later discover, Intuit's corporate headquarters in California has lodged an official bet that it can't be done. Blissfully unaware, and drawn by the prospect of applying approaches learned in previous earth-friendly projects to a commercial flagship, we sign on to lead the design.

Fast forward to Nov. 18, and indeed, the moving van pulls up at Intuit's new Canadian Headquarters on Edmonton's south side, depositing call centre gear in expansive quarters just before the phones kick into overdrive.

True, blowtorches still blaze elsewhere in the building—it'll be December before everyone makes the move. But the very fact that any part of the 95,000ft^2. (8600m^2) structure is open for business seems a miracle. What's more, this building promises to beat Canada's Model National Energy Code by 29.2 per cent, predicting savings of $65,000 a year in operating costs—despite fast-tracking, massive electronics and a plethora of creature comforts, proof positive that sustainable approaches can match the demands of 21st century enterprise. Putting it all together chalks up to be the most exciting adventure we've embarked on in recent years.

Rounding up the team.

Creating a team based on attitude and ability came naturally to Intuit, which relies on that same philosophy to earn its own success. It's an approach that also meshes perfectly with our style. But there's no doubt it breaks ranks with the more traditional construction model, which bases hiring decisions on lowest bid.

"We're the only weird and wonderful group that would say we could do this. Nobody else wanted to step up to the plate. A year after the fact, other contractors step up, saying 'We could have done it, too.'" *~Brian Robinson*

We proposed Clark Builders with whom we had worked with successfully in Russia as well as in Edmonton; fully 85 per cent of its recent projects involve construction management (architect and contractor working as a team). There's good reason to leave bottom-line bidding behind, says Brian Robinson, Clark Builders vice president of business development.

"We needed an architect with a track record of success. Somebody who'd been working in the global market—and somebody who could think out of the box." *~Nimal Rodrigo*

Clark Builders' own experience underlines the synergy created by a more collaborative style. "We're never shy about suggesting things that might improve a project," Robinson observes. "Not that we try to critique and pick architectural drawings apart, but often from standpoint of ease of construction, there's a better way or a more cost effective way of doing it."

Intuit's decision to build a team of trusted suppliers, all working for a negotiated fair price, proved crucial to everything that followed. As owner's agent, Atan Das saw that first-hand. "The whole project was all about having the right people with the right can-do attitude, able to think outside the box," he muses. "Because there was nothing about this project that I would call standard procedure."

Siting sidesteps.

In truth, most of us crossed our fingers in hope even as we assured Intuit its timeline could be met. Not only was this client seeking a monstrous and sophisticated building in six months…it hadn't even chosen a site.

Asked to provide some expert siting advice, both we and Clark Builders urged Intuit to minimize the challenges ahead by giving the nod to a nice level plot in a serviced research park. "In the back of my mind is this November deadline, and I'm trying to make life a little easier if I can," Brian Robinson says, chuckling at the memory. "But they wanted more of a tranquil setting."

Somewhere along the line, Intuit's leaders spotted just the place: a pastoral field near the scenic Mill Creek Ravine, abutting a spot slated by city planners for a pond, playing fields and trails. When I first looked at that site, all I could see were its challenges and complexities. The nine-acre plot sloped toward the ravine, a fact that complicated design; even more troublesome, it lay within 91 acres of farmland. Recently purchased by Consor Developers, the land had yet to be subdivided, let alone serviced. One of the early site alternative workshops explored these challenges—and I made the mistake of saying that we'd likely have to design a walk-out basement to make the building work on that site. Well, that was it—the Intuit team got excited about the possibilities and, picturing what the amenities right outside that door could mean for energetic young staff, chose the field over more "sensible" alternatives.

That late-May decision kicked action into high gear. We all knew the choice of site had instantly multiplied risks. And as so often happened in this project, events that ordinarily move in sequence occurred all at once, in a messy sort of parallel. "There was a whole regulatory process that hadn't even happened," Robinson recalls. "And we needed to start work immediately."

Recognizing Intuit as an ideal first tenant for its envisioned upscale business park, Consor Developers compressed its own timelines to seal the sale, promising the site would not only be subdivided and developed, but fully serviced by move-in. Inevitably, the work hit speed bumps, recalls Consor President Garry Stebner.

Fortunately, Edmonton's mayor and council realized the importance of keeping this high-tech headquarters in Edmonton, particularly in view of the fact that the region's economic blueprint places information and media services on a list of eight key growth clusters. Assured of support, civic administrators found informal ways to keep tabs while development and building permits were still winding through the system.

Having received approval to proceed based on little more than a concept plan, Stebner gave Intuit the go-ahead to come onsite in June, working around his own crews. As work sped ahead, he made sure to keep everyone, including city planners, in the loop. "It may have been nerve wracking for some people; at the time, there was a bit of overlap and frustration," he recalls. "But we proved the fast-track approach can work."

Running events in parallel raised its share of challenges. "Raised" is a particularly apt word for the earliest of those challenges: the migration of the building's allowable depth. Being near a ravine, we knew the building had to be high enough to avoid flooding, particularly since Edmonton intends to use the normally dry creek bed as a catch basin during large storms. Handling storm drainage on site was not yet something we had mastered. The creek presented challenges to design integration.

As might be expected in Alberta, weather played a role in elevating blood pressure. It rained the entire month of July. In mud up to our waists, we held daily site meetings to keep design and construction in sync. Then fall whizzed past, and winter threatened to descend before all parties had resolved the who-what-where of road construction and communication lines. "We didn't know whether Roper Road would be built in time," recalls Jack McCutcheon, Manasc Isaac project manager. "The road also affected getting services in, and Intuit couldn't have operated without those. Even cable was a big hassle at the end, who would run cable." Scheduled for completion in early September, the road was finally paved as October ended. "A week before it snowed," McCutcheon observes wryly. "We were that close to God getting us."

Many of us joined the nail-biting crew, wondering whether Intuit staff would jounce over rutted gravel all winter while running computers on temporary power. Not Consor's Stebner. "We would not have made that commitment had I not known we could do it," he says. It was a push, he acknowledges, ticking off the sewers, water mains, lights, roadway, signals and more—all completed in six months. "But Intuit is a super occupant, and they fit perfectly within our plans." Included in those plans is a top-of-bank walkway that will allow easy access to the woods and springtime water of the ravine, as well as the parkland next door.

It's now easy to see that the Mill Creek Ravine was the way to go. The new Intuit building fits hand-in-glove in its site at 7008 Roper Rd. Its walkout basement capitalizes on the natural slope, inviting staff to take meals from the cafeteria to the patio just outside, or perhaps step out for a stroll, a game of footbag, a quick spin on the bike. Expansion space, when needed, will connect with the building to create an enclosed courtyard.

Already, landscaping by award-winning Landscape Architect Doug Carlyle meshes with its surroundings to create a microclimate of sheltered exterior spaces. "The landscaping makes a wonderful complement to the building, like sitting in your backyard," observes designer Wes Sims. "And for these guys, that's what it is, because they're there all the time."

In the end, Intuit shifted its target move-in back three weeks to allow for the time lost in site selection. From our perspective as designers, the site is more than worth the delay. Not only does it fit Intuit's character, but its contour set the stage for innovative design, sustainable in its richest sense. As Sims notes, "To give the management credit, they wanted to be on that site. It's a bit rogue, and they're the first in that area, so they've set the tone. They're not just another building in another park. It was more work for everyone, but it gave staff the best amenities. And for us, it was an exciting roller coaster ride."

Workshops inform design.

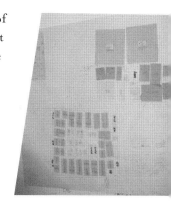

Extensive client workshops have become a Manasc Isaac trademark, part of our sustainability bible. Given the speed required by the Intuit project, one might assume those workshops would fall by the wayside, skipped in the race toward the finish line. But past experience tells us that hours spent listening to clients at the early stages can save days of backtracking during construction, when the stakes are higher. Only by listening could we create a building that meets the needs of the people working there, and thus will remain sustainable for the long term. So we led multiple workshops, inviting Intuit staff to crystallize their vision of the place and describe that vision to us. At the same time, we took advantage of those workshops to model and describe our integrated approach to design, bringing key design and construction decision maker together in Manasc Isaac offices every Monday from noon to 8 p.m.

"We don't have time not to do workshops. Every project starts with the client 'Who do we have in the box? 'Who is this person?' That's a fundamental starting point. We don't potato stamp buildings. Our next building won't look like this, because the next client will not be like this." ~*Wes Sims*

To achieve maximum value from the client workshops, our designers enter the process with open minds. "We have a lot of ideas we want to incorporate, including sustainability, but we really have no preconceptions about colours or materials or systems," says Wes Sims. "It's through the workshops that I get my sense of who the client is. Every technical decision stems from that initial contact. It's critical for us."

Acutely aware of the correlation between satisfied staff and quality work, Intuit gave the workshop process full support. "We have a fairly young, high tech workforce, and we wanted to outfit this place with whatever they need to be creative," says Intuit Controller Nimal Rodrigo, who played a lead role in the entire project.

Yet our inclusive approach to workplace design was somewhat foreign to staff members. "In their old space, they had an interior decorator do everything, and it was all very quiet, in beige and blue," recalls designer Deana MacKenzie. "At first, they wanted us to just show up with something they'd all love. We told them, 'You can participate; after all, this is where you'll be living.'"

With as many as twenty people involved in the workshops, consensus sometimes seemed doubtful. But as Sims says, "At the end of the day, they know it's their building, not something somebody built for them."

"Given the diversity of what people thought they wanted, Vivian and her crew had some work to do, to get down to a style that everybody was going to be happy with." ~*Nimal Rodrigo*

Exterior personality.

One look at the Intuit exterior reveals volumes about what we heard in those workshops. "They didn't want the standard beige, monolithic looking building, and they wanted the feel of stone," recalls Sims, who stickhandled exterior design. In the end, budget and time constraints precluded adding masonry to the mix, but designers managed to evoke the feel of stone by incorporating darkened concrete block at pedestrian level. Above those blocks, contrasting stucco in golden hues is offset by splashes of red, creating lively focal points at the places where people naturally gather. "We used colours to warm up the outdoor people areas," Sims explains. Ample landscaping makes those areas even more inviting, he adds, and for good reason. "They plan on using the outside of the building a lot."

Indeed, the building sports five balconies and two patios, giving each team ready access to the outdoors. What's more, those spots are equipped with gas for barbecues and radiant heat, plus smokeless ash trays. "In a lot of projects those are the first things to go, and the whole building gets boxed in," Sims says. "To its credit, Intuit never gave those up." Quite the contrary: Intuit was first to suggest running gas outdoors.

Perhaps it helped that the project team's weekly marathons used the Manasc Isaac boardroom, overlooking a roof-top deck that attracted a near-constant parade of smokers, sun seekers and impromptu meetings. "When we sat in these design meetings and they saw things like that, they said, 'Yeah, we need this,'" recalls Jack McCutcheon, Manasc Isaac project manager. What they saw was not a lie, he adds. "I don't think we could survive without our outdoor space anymore. "Barely had Intuit moved into its new home than its patios and balconies became equally well used, magnets for solo and group pursuits, work as well as play.

Interior palette.

With its curved feature walls and purple accents, Intuit Canada's interior space also embodies what we learned about its unconventional staff. "The design is somewhat whimsical, and that reflects the open nature of the organization. It's not corporate, not conservative or strict by any means," says Sandra Valens, who joined Manasc Isaac just in time to become immersed in the Intuit panic.

"A number of staff have come up to me as I've been doing site visits to say 'I really like working here—it feels like home.' That's good to hear." *~Sandra Valens*

The indoor colour scheme alone was the subject of many long meetings, recalls Deana MacKenzie, who worked with Valens on interior design. Staff helped set parameters by identifying existing furniture and corporate colours that needed to be woven into the palette—and by expressing distinct dislikes. "We had a big green issue," MacKenzie says, making a long story short. "Green was not the colour of choice."

Informed by a dozen department leaders and numerous other voices, the palette grew to more than 10 colours, including some that were questioned as too strident and clashing. In an inspired moment, MacKenzie brought in a bouquet of flowers sprayed to match those diverse hues, providing 3-D visuals for a decision that is often based on 2-D colour chips.

Fear of colour clash occurred in part because staff couldn't quite grasp the immensity of their new home, MacKenzie notes. "They would say, 'It's no bigger than what we have now,' and we'd say 'But it is. Five times bigger.'" With a scale so large, it was not only possible, but appropriate to create distinct character in different areas, she adds. "Considering that this a building where people spend more than an eight-hour day, we wanted to create diverse spaces, so there's not one colour scheme throughout the entire place. And we tried to come up with a scheme that was lively, more exciting than the normal whites."

The final palette, reached many iterations after those initial workshops, uses purple as a dominant accent, balanced with warm colours such as yellow and ochre. The palette does include green, but not hospital green; rather, a hue that connects to the external life that's so much a part of this crew's life.

The entire process of colouring their space gave staff liberty to explore, MacKenzie adds. "People who at the beginning were very scared by the bold colours ended up putting them in their own offices. Now staff are adding their own coloured pieces."

Soft touches.

Walking through the building with Intuit's Rodrigo, it's clear the creativity purchased to design innovative software has rubbed off in the planning of its new home. Mounting stairs from the spacious lobby, Rodrigo notes with satisfaction that the stairwell door (required for both fire safety and intellectual security) rests at a midpoint landing, allowing an open feel at both bottom and top floors. As we wander past large windows, he points out that they're positioned to allow natural light into a section of the building whose own exterior wall is blocked by yet another staircase. Opening the door into a half gymnasium, home to volleyball, floor hockey and other athletic pursuits, he notes that the gym serves double duty as the one spot large enough for full-staff meetings. Such space-maximizing ideas percolated from staff; equally important, they were heard by leaders who recognize the value of catering to individuals who create as they play.

The gym is far from alone among the building's take-a-break amenities. Sprinkled among offices are sleep rooms, fully endorsed for snoring on the job. On the lower level, you'll find an impressive fitness centre, a fireplace lounge with billiards and such—and a gourmet cafeteria. Like the gym, many of those spots double as informal work stations. A bean bag room, for example, is wired for laptops.

Intuit's code:
1. Integrity without compromise 2. Do right by all our customers 3. It's the people 4. Seek the best
5. Continually improve processes 6. Speak, listen and respond 7. Teams work 8. Customers define quality
9. Think fast, move fast 10. We care and give back

The cafeteria itself illustrates how the entire team worked together to turn challenges into assets. The site's natural slope, which originally made us all nervous about this land, opened the door quite literally to a walkout entrance, complete with large windows overlooking a patio and the ravine beyond. Recognizing the cafeteria's importance for a staff that works (and brainstorms) through mealtimes, Intuit requested a full kitchen, equipped for the discerning palate and health-conscious body. Finishing touches are high quality, from bounce lighting (rather than the traditional cafeteria glare) to linoleum floors, cut into swirls of colour for a look-good, feel-good, long-lasting covering. As Valens notes, "This cafeteria could have been a simple utilitarian space, but it turned out to be quite a focal point of the whole building."

Flexible spaces.

Beyond creature comforts, design workshops highlighted emerging strategic needs in this rapidly expanding firm. Among those needs: a training room for call centre employees, who are hired by the dozens to gear up for peak seasons such as tax time; a fully digital audio visual room, capable of portraying Intuit's strengths; acoustic privacy for engineers working on proprietary software; numerous breakout rooms, where teams can crank up the synergy.

As that list implies, we heard a strong preference for group space, a distinct departure from the North American love affair with personal domain. Consequently, each person's individual space is not large; many of the 350 staff members work in portable cubicles just as they had in Intuit's previous quarters. While constrained by the need to reuse existing cubicles, we were careful to heed Intuit's request that the units be grouped by team, with each team loosely enclosed by physical boundaries. "We tried to give each of our departments a very open feeling, but we used walls to segregate each team," Intuit's Rodrigo says. "In a massive space that's totally open, you're not going to have that team feeling."

We also invited staff to customize their layouts. The main floor, for example, sports extra-tall cubicles, some of which open to each other to create work pods. Engineers live here. As Rodrigo explains, "They really like their quiet and privacy, but they also need to consult." Like all the pods, these can easily be reconfigured as teams evolve.

In a building designed to hold as many as 450 individuals, it was important to create a logical way-finding system, Valens notes. "It's almost like designing a city, with main freeways, smaller roads and residential streets. But there's nothing worse than a whole building of cubicles. So we created this curved wall to locate the public amenities, such as coffee areas, washrooms and large meeting rooms." Randomly placed accent squares echo the colour in the wall, calling attention to those curves.

Unusual angles add to the appeal. On one floor, cubicles march at an angle; on another, the lights or carpet tiles cut an angular swath. It's all intentional, all part of a logical playfulness that emulates the Intuit culture. Very subtly, without overdoing it, we've used line and colour to break up the geometry of the space.

Call centre.

Workshops with call centre staff alerted us that this huge segment of the building posed a particular design challenge. As staff described their lives "inside the telephone," we realized they need space not so much on desktops as around their heads, to counterbalance those disembodied conversations.

To provide that ambience, we designed a massive, high-ceilinged area. Seated around carousels that evoke space pods, workers have minimal elbow room, but their eyes can roam great reaches of space. Offices and meeting rooms perched midway to the ceiling emphasize the room's height, while skylights and high windows bring in natural light at an angle designed to avoid glare on computer screens.

The call centre has its own culture and is spatially independent, its orientation skewed and its entry deliberately separate due to the proprietary nature of the software being developed elsewhere in the building. That separation gave designers licence to play with a slightly different palette of colours here, accented by a rich red that contrasts well with the wooden trusses holding up the huge span.

Walking through the cavernous space now, there's a buzz of conversation as staff assist far-flung clients in multiple languages. Reflecting a concern for acoustic privacy that's present throughout the building, the sound is masked by white noise. Initially set quite high, that piped-in noise has been slowly reduced to a volume that aims to blur voices without being intrusive. As we're discovering in this space and elsewhere, however, achieving optimum acoustic privacy is a tricky proposition when working with a client ever vigilant about both setting the stage for creativity and keeping its intellectual property out of the wrong hands.

Imbedded sustainability.

Sustainability is built in to Intuit Canada's headquarters. Besides consuming 29 per cent less energy than a comparable building designed to the benchmark of the model national energy code, the facility promises savings of $65,000 a year in operating costs, coupled with significantly reduced greenhouse gas emissions. All those benefits, plus comfort for staff and users.

At great cost? Hardly. We managed to improve the performance of Intuit's new headquarters without inflating capital costs above the $14.4 million budget. The careful modelling required for sustainability did impact design costs. But those expenses were recovered through Canada's Commercial Building Incentive Program.

It's crucial to note, however, that our success depended on an integrated "whole building" approach. Simply adding bells and whistles (or subtracting window area, as in the '70s attempt at saving energy) would almost certainly have escalated costs without creating a sustainable building. Instead, selections made throughout the entire structure—walls, windows, roof, lighting, mechanical system, adhesives, finishes, flooring—were integrated to optimize performance. Similarly, we viewed costs from a broader perspective rather than line-by-line, realizing that the expense of an innovative access flooring system, for example, would be recouped in part by the ease of running electrical and mechanical systems under that floor. Thus the need for all involved to work as a focused team, cross-fertilizing solutions in a relationship that invited excellence.

Research on earlier projects allowed us to persuade the Intuit team that sustainable strategies work. An issue of Environmental Building News from January of 1998 provided the story on the access floor. This article paved the way for the support needed to use the access floor in Intuit's office and call centre.

There's no doubt that sustainable approaches add a layer of complexity. Because a healthy building embodies nested criteria, each decision must make sense not only on its own, but in relation to the whole. Windows, for example, can't be planned in isolation, but in the context of interior walls, mechanical systems and other details affecting the flow of air and light throughout the building. But as our designers readily attest, that upfront effort reaps a lasting result: a building that's better for its owners, its environment and its users. Our marathon weekly meetings, coupled with a daily blizzard of conversations, enabled us to make the critical trade-offs that enhance sustainability while keeping costs in check.

Indeed, this sustainability agenda differs from the '70s brand of energy efficiency not only in its focus on integration but also in its attention to user comfort.

Excerpts from
Environmental Building News™
Volume 7, Number 1 January 1998

"Simply put, access flooring is a winner. Long used in computer rooms, access floors are now finding their way into office buildings and other commercial space, where they can dramatically reduce renovation costs while saving energy and improving indoor air quality—especially when providing an underfloor plenum for conditioned air distribution."

"...With access flooring, the construction schedule for electrical rough-ins can often be more flexible because the wires are readily accessible. Also, because floor modules with outlets and cable jacks can be located anywhere in the floor, it may be possible to get by without electrified furniture (furniture with integral cable trays and wiring). This can reduce furniture costs by $1000 per workstation..."

"Delivery of conditioned air at the floor level also means that the air doesn't need to be as cold. Conventional HVAC systems in commercial buildings deliver air at about 13°C, while the supply air can be as warm as 17°C in access-floor-delivery systems. this is possible because the conditioned air is delivered in the occupied zone of the room and because the delivered air does not pick up heat from the lights near the ceiling, as occurrs with ceiling air supply. The upward air flow carries away unwanted heat before it reaches the occupied space."

"The extra cost of the access flooring was $8 per square foot ($86/m^2), but when other costs relating to finishes, conditioned air distribution, and wiring systems are included in the comparison, the access flooring system actually saves $2.70 per square foot ($29/m^2) in construction cost."

Daylight and energy.

Choosing mechanical and electrical consultants who share the sustainable vision and bringing them to the table immediately proved essential to conserving energy in the Intuit building —and indeed, to overall success. "We were involved at the very start, and that's the whole secret of sustainable design," says Grice, who provided electrical expertise while Chris Jepson of Keen Engineering Co. Ltd. designed mechanical systems. "We came on two weeks after the architects. In a normal project, we wouldn't be brought on until much later. But the very first step of siting a building can have major impact on how much energy is needed in addition to the sun."

Placing the building on Intuit's chosen lot proved relatively straightforward, given the expertise at hand. By happy coincidence, the north-south orientation that allows best solar exposure also provides ideal views toward the nearby ravine. "Normally, we would do a solar analysis and fine-tune plans to get a perfect orientation, but with Intuit we didn't have time," Grice recalls. Instead, the building's placement was based on a decade of sustainable experience. Subsequent computer modelling shows that 30 per cent more daylight enters the building than first calculated, a major feat given the structure's massive floor plate. "It's hard to get that perimeter lighting all the way in," Grice explains. "But if you just walk into the building, regardless of the orientation of the sun, you'll see a lot of natural light."

"Natural light for us was huge. We wanted everybody in the building to see it."

That's exactly what workers asked for, says Controller Nimal Rodrigo. The north-south orientation also maximizes the inflow of heat, which is soaked up by the building's mass to provide winter warming.

On the downside, streams of sunlight can create glare and hot spots at certain times of the day, a particular concern in an environment saturated with computer screens. "Actually, the secret is not necessarily getting an awful lot of daylighting into the building. The secret is using solar shades and light shelves to filter the sunlight, so most of the light bounces off ceiling," Grice explains. Ideally, external shades stop not only glare, but unwanted heat gain, he adds. "That's the concept, and you've got to get it right. If you don't, all the work you do to get sunlight into the building is mitigated by the fact that people cover the windows with cardboard boxes. There's some science to it, but also some art."

The Intuit building uses exterior solar shades on all but the north side, where light enters at an oblique angle that is perfect for indoor use. "Fortunately, we were working with enlightened designers (pardon the pun) who worked with us to make sure the light shelf becomes an architectural statement as well as a functional engineering piece."

"A building that really understands what solar gain is all about will have different solar control on each side." ~Tony Grice

Sustainable devices such as window shades hark back to historic buildings in Europe and South America, Grice notes, and that's no accident. "We're going back to simple things people have done for centuries, when they didn't have air conditioning and electric lights. We're borrowing ideas from the past."

Yet our engineers are equally focused on the future—a time, they say, when buildings will have inbuilt capacity to respond to the sun rather than relying on the people inside to open and close mechanical contraptions. Already, some buildings automatically "don the sunglasses" when glazing detects strong glare. Cost constraints precluded that level of automation in the Intuit building, putting onus on staff to optimize energy use.

Whether self-propelled or occupant-assisted, solar awareness will soon be essential in an industry scrambling to beat rising energy costs, Grice predicts. In fact, rising prices, coupled with increasingly sophisticated modelling software, are finally attracting client attention to techniques Grice and Jepson have been honing for 10 years. "It's becoming easier and easier to sell our approach on pure energy savings," Grice says. "Suddenly, you can see that daylighting is key to meeting energy targets. If you get it right, the initial cost is the same or soon outweighed by energy savings. Rather than 'That would be nice to do,' the response becomes 'We'd better do this.'"

Intuit's sustainable elements.

Integrated, Embedded, Enjoyed

- **Site:**
  Designed to create a microclimate of sheltered outdoor spaces. Lunchroom with outdoor patio located on southwest corner for evening use. Access to Mill creek ravine for recreational activities, bicycle trails and walkways.
- **Orientation:**
  Views to the ravine for individual offices. Design reduces heat and glare from the low summer sun to the west. Shading devices on west and east sides reduce heat gain.
- **Operable Windows:**
  Sized and placed to maximize daylight and reduce energy use; openers allow local ventilation and individual control.
- **Materials:**
  Conventional and engineered wood chosen for high-speed construction, aesthetic qualities and low embodied energy. Linoleum and carpet tile floors and other finishes chosen for maximum durability and minimum impact on indoor air quality and reduced environmental impact.
- **Building envelope:**
  Exterior sheathing, "peel & stick" membrane, exterior insulation and acrylic stucco in a rainscreen assembly. Windows are vinyl framed and sealed to the wall membrane. Glazing low E-coated and gas filled.
- **Comfort:**
  Accessible, floor-based air delivery system optimizes comfort as well as energy performance.
- **Lighting:**
  High quality, energy efficient direct/indirect lighting in all workspaces. Lots of daylight!
- **Climate change:**
  Achieves greater than 29 percent reduction of greenhouse gas emissions compared to a conventional building.
- **Capital and operating costs:**
  No increased capital cost to improve building performance; incremental design cost covered by CPIB funds; savings of $65,000 a year in reduced operating cost.

Everything old, new again:
Ancient wisdom, quantified

Manasc: Our ability to predict the performance of a building is huge—really a leap forward. Unless we can with some confidence predict, not just based on intuition, but quantifiably say, 'We should be able to achieve this,' the whole sustainability agenda falls apart. In the old days, doing full building energy simulation modeling was like designing airplanes by hand: not really worth doing, way too much work.

Emery Yakowich: It was easier to build one and see if it would fly, like the Wright brothers—and risk a few crashing.

Manasc: Why wouldn't you, if it would take 10 million hours to calculate it or 10,000 hours to build one and test it. Buildings were like that; there was good knowledge out there years ago, but the ability to model, the ability to simulate, hasn't been around very long.

Yakowich: Evolution was trial and error. That cathedral lasted 1000 years, this one 200, so that one must be better.

Manasc: And of course infloor heating systems and atria, all the stuff we think of today as being state of the art, was well known in Roman times, thousands of years ago. But nobody had the data to prove it. That was okay in Roman times; the master builders built it, and that's how it was. But in this scientific era, architecture finds itself trying to catch up with the world of science. And the horsepower of computers to be able to prove sustainability to people in the scientific paradigm in any kind of cost-effective way is really quite new. As recently as the '90s, software for energy modelling was scarce and expensive. Once we got started on Intuit and I had committed to a sustainable result I realized that we would have trouble modelling the performance in the time available. With so many decisions already made, would the modelling even make sense? I called Gord Shymko and begged to get a DOE. 2 model done for the project really quickly. Thankfully, Gord came through—but early results suggested that, even with a good building envelope and access floor air delivery, we might have challenges. The deep floor plate was less than ideal. We had to modify the zones under the access floor. Finally modelling results were complete and the building was well underway. We could achieve 29% savings.

Grice: Intuitively, we could make the same predictions, because we've done enough of these projects and the latitude doesn't change that much. Take building orientation, for example; there's only a 360-degree field in which you can work, so after awhile, it's pretty intuitive. But the fact that we can sit down with a client and give something with four decimal places in it just raises their level of confidence. So it's much easier to substantiate; easier to quantify, which is really important.

Manasc: On one level, it's really important; on another level, it's completely trivial. In a sense, we live in a world caught between two worlds. Really, the art of design hasn't changed; the way a designer in Rome designed an aqueduct is absolutely no different. And they work and they're beautiful. But on the other hand, everything is new because we're now in this funny world of everything being quantifiable. The 21st century world of science (which is a fiction—it's really a world of humans) says the world of building is left behind. And it is, except for the sustainable building piece. The sustainable design agenda is a bridge between the two, between art and science. We're out there in the world of science; we can quantify and measure.

Grice: My peers will phone me up and say, 'Tony, this green sustainable thing. This is a great marketing idea. Just the same stuff we've been doing for years, right? But you've got a new name for it.' They could never be bothered to stretch it. In the past, we've been paid according to however much we could consume in capital dollars, and even energy. The bigger machines we could put into building, the more we got paid. And that's the culture of our industry. We can all say we're professionals and always do the best for our clients. The real truth is that the only way you survive as a consultant, particularly in tough times, is to make money. And the only way you make money, if fees are based on the size of machine you put into a building, is to put in big machines. That's why there are a lot of buildings with big machines in them. That's the culture, and that's why we have to change. Because we have to put in no machines, or tiny machines—and still get paid for the value of understanding how to get to no machines. Maybe it goes back to the aqueducts. Maybe the aqueducts are lined with Teflon now. Whatever the little bit of technology is, that understanding is the value we bring. Not the ability to specify big machines.

Windows on the world.

As might be predicted from the desire to maximize daylight, windows figure large in the Intuit design. Large, opening, properly glazed windows that maximize daylight, minimize energy use and increase comfort.

"Sealed boxes were a very brave experiment, on a very large scale. Before the 1970's, nobody had sealed buildings; after 2010, nobody will have sealed boxes either. From 1970 to 2010 in the grand scheme of history isn't a huge time. So it's a 40-year brave experiment brought on by air conditioning that has largely failed."

We're fully aware that our approach differs markedly from the last wave of energy efficiency, which saw windows as bad, and shrank them—in some cases, to nothing. Frankly, the culprit wasn't so much windows as overall poor design, coupled with ineffective building envelopes. As the windows shrank, so too did the quality of the environments inside. Just ask the children trying to study in schools that lost sunlight through the retrofits of the '70s.

The fact that we use operable rather than sealed windows also sets us apart from the norm on today's commercial and institutional building scene. Think about it: When have you last seen an office building the size of Intuit's new headquarters with anything but sealed windows? Yet a short walk through history reveals that sealed windows have been with us mere decades. Sealed-tight buildings do simplify life for mechanical engineers, but as we've discovered in workshops with Intuit and many other clients, they leave the humans inside starved for fresh air and a sense of connection with the outdoors. Today, that desire is compounded by growing concern about the possible health effects of sealed environments, including diseases caused by mould and poor air quality.

"One of the biggest things you'll notice right away are our windows. Natural light for us was huge. So we have operable windows that are nice and big." ~Nimal Rodrigo

Not that we create every window equal. Quite the contrary. Each window's high performance glazing, like its shading treatment, is determined by its orientation, to achieve balanced solar gain.

In Intuit's call centre, windows are set high above, to minimize the potential of glare on the ever-present computer screens. Meeting rooms, by contrast, sport large windows that extend close to the floor, and open at bottom for maximum connection with the energizing outdoors. Upstairs, where desks predominate, openers are at top, to minimize the worry that papers will blow around. In short, the windows mesh our knowledge of daylight with what we've learned about Intuit's people and how they'll use their space.

Bounced light.

Augmenting the natural feel brought by sunlight is a lighting system that bounces fully 95 per cent of the wattage off the ceiling. That indirect lighting creates a soft, shadowless glow, quite different from the glare that produces furrowed brows and tight necks in most offices.

"One of the biggest things that came out of our workshops was people's desire to not get killed by fluorescent lighting," says Intuit's Rodrigo. To select the lighting, the Intuit staff, design team and lighting suppliers toured about six different installations around Edmonton. It took many conversations to agree on the overall approach of 90% up light and 10% down light. The balance between the comfort of people looking at screens, walking around and other activities kept the discussion lively. Then we had to order the light fixtures. Intuit is far from alone; realization is growing that liveable lighting is key to worker productivity, particularly in electronics-dominated environments. In fact, notes Grice, who designed Intuit's lighting, surveys by Cornell University and others indicate that staff in today's most common workstation-heavy workplace fear eye strain even more than asbestos or snakes or cockroaches. "It's inherent in the human species to be affected by light."

"I was asked to go back because Intuit was concerned the lighting levels were reading low. We have flexibility to easily go in and change lighting and air distribution, but the secret is not to arbitrarily adjust the levels if they haven't quite met external standards. It's the human element you adjust systems to." *~Tony Grice*

Bright, uniform overhead lighting can cause an adrenaline rush, Grice adds. "So it's no wonder stores use very bright ceilings; they want you to come in, quickly buy whole bunch of stuff, then get out as fast as possible." Such lighting uses high wattage to compensate for poor design. Like a gardener spraying water directly at a plant, Grice explains, "you've got to drive a whole bunch down, because some of it will splash back up." A gentle mist, by contrast, can accomplish more with less. Ditto bounce lighting: Intuit's wattage is less than half the 750-LUX standard set by many government departments. As Grice says, "You don't design lighting for light meters. You design it for the people who occupy the space."

Access Floor.

Once living in the building, staff realized the underfloor system requires a break-in period. "It's like a new car," says Jepson. "Maybe it doesn't feel the same, and it may not be adjusted quite right. But at least with operable windows and underfloor air systems, you give people the opportunity to change the way air is supplied around them."

"Everybody's different; you may want lots of air, somebody else wants little. People are happier when they have some control over their space." *~Chris Jepson*

"People wanted the ability to control temperature. So we've got a grill you actually move around to change the temperature of your work station. The person who runs our facility force can remove that square of carpet tile and move it somewhere else, and put a grill there instead." *~Nimal Rodrigo*

When proposing this unconventional system, our consulting engineers arranged a team visit to BC Hydro, which built two towers a decade ago, one with underfloor air, the other with conventional systems. A retired building supervisor served as our tour guide, happy to illustrate the "night and day" difference between the two towers. The underfloor system, he said, has proven less troublesome to operate and more conducive to comfort.

Our team, meanwhile, was struck by differences among work stations in the tower fitted with an access floor. "It was amazing to see how one person would have three grills circling the desk, while another had no grills nearby at all," Jepson says. "Everybody has a different metabolic rate. Rather than fighting the people working inside the building, this system buys into it. When you give back control to the individual, rather than saying 'Don't touch anything,' people are happier.

Intuit's entire floor is raised 18 inches, on a grid that allows easy access to the cavity below. Under 24-inch squares of carpet runs the morass of wires, cables and pipes needed for a high tech office, plus air for temperature control. The air emerges through grills or diffusers scattered about the floor; staff can increase or diminish their personal airflow by dictating the placement of diffusers around their work stations.

Access flooring simplifies the task of sending air to the centre of the building, notes Intuit Vice President Chad Frederick. "In a typical building with a central fan and heating/cooling system, you need to plumb ducts or individual ductwork to each place within the floor that you want to have airflow." To save money, those ducts often concentrate along the exterior, leaving staff in the centre less well served. "With access flooring, one of the benefits, and we're seeing it here, is that it's easier to send a more consistent and non-stop airflow to the interior the building. Not at a high pressure, but high volume and low pressure. To me, that's the number one benefit of access flooring."

"The access floor was different. I had done computer rooms that way, but not a complete floor. It was new to me, and quite slick." ~Dave Wardrop

The decision to use access flooring also injected flexibility into our design process, a key factor in this hyper-tracked project. "We were still designing interior departments while the building was going up," notes designer Wes Sims. "The access floor gave us the ability to not worry about where walls and electrical and plumbing were going, as we could integrate those at the last moment, from below." Even after construction is complete, those systems can be moved from below as uses shift, increasing the building's ability to adapt—and thus its potential for long life.

Earth-friendly materials.

For a commercial building such as Intuit, the specifications fill a fat binder. From paint to adhesive, from varnish to carpet, here is our chance to ensure that the structure is sustainable to its core. We've built a full library of sustainably aware suppliers in the past decade, and those suppliers make it their business to keep us informed about earth-friendly options.

Take flooring, for example. In the Intuit building, carpet covers much of the floor. Carpet is not always the sustainable flooring of choice, since it can all too easily off-gas toxins and attract germs and mould. But like most offices, Intuit needed the quiet and comfort offered by sound-absorbing flooring. So we chose carpet tile, but were very particular about specifying sustainable carpet. Both carpet and backing are fully recyclable and designed not to release noxious gases. Also, the carpet is laid in tiles, allowing worn spots to be replaced in patches rather than entire rolls. Use of tiles also opened the door to a scattering of bright accent tiles that add a touch of whimsy to the scene.

In the cafeteria, where the need for quiet gives way to other concerns, we chose linoleum, which withstands long, hard wear. Furthermore, the type we chose is made of cork and linseed oil, rapidly renewable resources, rather than petroleum, which releases volatile organics into the indoor environment.

"Flooring is one element of a building that is changed most often," notes designer Sandra Valens. "So some flooring manufacturers have really stepped up to bat, and made sure their materials are sustainable. When you look at the millions of tons that could go into landfills, it only makes sense."

Just enough.

"We design so there's just enough, because that will be the most efficient system you can possibly get," says Keen Engineering's Jepson. For engineers dealing with the heating, cooling and electrical systems we all depend on, "just enough" demands a paradigm shift, he adds. "In the past, we've said, 'What happens if it's not quite built as it should be? We'd better build in some safety margins.' It's the North American way, but it's a waste."

Like Jepson, Tony Grice views buildings such as the Intuit headquarters as a step toward structures that will actually add power back into the grid rather than consuming power. "We're trying to make systems simpler and work more naturally with the environment rather than throwing a bunch of technology at the building," he says. Our ultimate goal is to design a building that does not have a mechanical system and that is 100 per cent naturally lit during the day."

As a trade-off for saving energy and money, staff may need to wear a sweater or shed a layer when extremes strike, Jepson adds. "If you hit certain peaks, such as the darkest day of the year or a very very hot day, nobody notices in all those buildings designed with extra capacity," he notes. "But if people are prepared to give up a little bit on those extreme days, that allows you to be far more flexible. And if people are part of the decision and understand why, and if they know they can open a window or move vents around, they will buy into that concept and become part of making that overall building sustainable."

Wood framed.

One of the first discussions at our full-team Monday afternoon work sessions focused on the all-too-tight schedule. What must be pre-ordered, when did we need particular materials onsite, what sequence of design and construction activities could we contemplate? At that first session, with structural engineers, contractors, project managers and clients at the table, I asked the question people have come to expect from us: "What about wood? Could this be a wood building?" At first, the whole team doubted the sense of using wood to frame a structure whose massive size would usually dictate steel. But then the ideas came tumbling out. Unlike steel, which must be ordered months in advance in specific sizes, engineered wood products are immediately available and easy to adjust on site. Maybe wood really did make sense—if Intuit could live with 6m spans in the offics interior. Given the desire to define team boundaries with visual dividers, Intuit leaders responded that smaller spans would be fine. By the end of that meeting, we'd decided on a wood building with six-metre spans.

In retrospect, that decision was key to meeting Intuit's hyper-tracked timeline. "Because we knew there were lots of things we didn't know, we had to have maximum flexibility," notes designer Wes Sims. "With wood, we could move that window around. If we had done this as a steel building, those design changes would have cost us." Steel was used for the building's supporting columns, he added, and in the end, many columns required adjustment on site.

Thank goodness we didn't use steel joists, which are much harder than columns to modify. The post-and-beam design used for the wood frame structure also facilitated speedy assembly, notes Aftab Jessa, Clark Builders' senior estimator. "You erect your columns, just plunk in the beams, put in joists and the building is up. Then all the outside walls are in-filled with prefabricated panels. It went up like a Meccano set."

"We're not the only architects in Alberta doing wood buildings, but we're the only ones who systematically, over 20 years, have chosen wood as a structural material over other alternatives. We do that for a lot of reasons–partly economics, partly expediency, but also sustainability."

Clark Builders' superintendent Dave Wardrop still prefers building with steel, which requires fewer columns. But even he acknowledges wood made sense for the Intuit headquarters. "We needed instant materials off the shelf in just about every aspect of the project. And generally, the grid is not too bad," he allows. "The columns we used are six inches maximum, so they didn't take up too much space."

Fast-track integration.

Without a doubt, the Intuit headquarters is the fastest project ever undertaken by Manasc Isaac Architects. The six months between May 25, when Intuit selected the site, and Nov. 18, when move-in began, flew past in an intense blur of non-stop action. Driven by economy and speed, yet shooting for sustainability, we constantly juggled materials and methods to make the Intuit equation work.

"I don't want to do another one of these this year. But call next year, and we'll talk." ~Emery Yakowich

I remember sitting in Nimal Rodrigo's office in the old Intuit workplace and imagining how we could make this building happen. It was an enormous stretch, given that he was asking for two years' work in six months. The risk was huge. We succeeded, quite frankly, by doing nearly everything at once. Along the way, we broke all the conventions of architectural practice and tested everything I've learned in 25 years.

The fact that we began each week with a high-level meeting of the minds became crucial. Those Monday sessions filled the Manasc Isaac meeting room to the brim not only with bodies, but with a palpable sense of synergy. All key players attended, together making the on-the-spot decisions needed in a timeline that allowed no second-guessing.

"In the team, it's important that the end user identifies exactly what is top priority. For Intuit, because of product launch dates, the crucial issue was scheduling. So we weighed every decision against that," *~Atan Das*

Those meetings also proved essential for Aftab Jessa, Clark Builders' senior estimator. "That's where I started building a mental picture of the building," he recalls. "They had a vision of what the job would be, which enabled me to do proper budgeting." Engineers were particularly helpful, for example, in budgeting the under-floor mechanical system, a first for Clark Builders, and possibly for Alberta.

"You need a huge amount of people working on a project like that, and you need commitment that everybody stays with the project until it's finished. Vivian threw a lot of resources at project, and so did Clark. Otherwise, we'd still be doing sketches." *~Jack McCutcheon*

From its very beginning, the project attracted many astonished looks. Perhaps the first came from an excavator, called out to dig a basement only to learn he couldn't refer to the plans, because at the moment, there were none. "He looked at me like I was crazy," recalls Terry Richelhoff, Clark Builders construction manager. "I said, 'Just start digging, and I'll tell you when to quit.'"

"This is the fastest project we have ever

"There was a vast pool of experience around

done. It put a huge amount of onus on

the table, and we could draw on each other.

everyone to really ride it hard, with

People were there who could visualize

never a day off. That made it exciting,

problems and troubleshoot ahead." ~*Atan Das*

even though it was really intense."

Intuit's hyper-tracked schedule.

May 3, 2000 : Vision workshop, site alternatives

May 8, 2000: Contractor/design team at design workshop, sustainable vision

May 12, 2000: Program workshop

May 15, 2000: First cost plan

May 25, 2000: Site selection

May 26, 2000: Building footprint approved

June 1, 2000: Development permit drawing submitted

June 11, 2000: Team meets to cut costs

June 12, 2000: Data Centre design

June 14, 2000: Detailed planning and design review

June 20, 2000: Foundation permit drawings submitted

June 22, 2000: Ground breaking

June 26, 2000: Mechanical and electrical equipment ordered, sustainable design strategy integrated, including energy modelling

August, 2000: Framing

November 1, 2000: Cladding

October 4, 2000: Interiors

January 31, 2001: Official opening

Design constructing.

For Manasc Isaac designers racing to keep ahead of the hammers, Intuit was a project with a unique drama line. A full 10 of us, more than a third of the staff, threw ourselves into the fray, working double shifts and weekends to move the design along.

"My purpose is contract administration, and since we didn't have documents at the beginning, and no specifications, and sketchy drawings, it all started out rather loosely," recalls Jack McCutcheon. "I'm the site contact, and normally I have documents to reference when they start asking questions, but this was a completely different way of doing a construction project. The only way I could find anything out was to talk to Emery."

Indeed, Manasc Isaac technologist Emery Yakowich earns high praise from the entire team for drawing up plans at warp speed. Busy juggling people and problems each day, he holed up nights and weekends to, as McCutcheon puts it, "get this stuff out of his brain and down on computer."

Fortunately, our designers can depend on Yakowich to not only transcribe but improve unusual concepts. "There's a danger in going from design to construction documents that the intention gets lost, but with Emery, it doesn't," says Wes Sims. "Emery understands the architectural intent, and he expects us to throw curves."

Recalling how he tried in vain to stay "one step beyond Jack, at least a day ahead," Yakowich admits the monstrous hours tested his family's patience. Yet he welcomed the challenge of creating a signature building rather than "the cookie cutter approach, because that is boring."

Far from cookie-cutter, Intuit design continued to evolve as the client's own needs clarified. "Intuit was still making programming decisions while the building was going up, so things were extremely fluid," recalls Sims. "If you wanted to move a window, you had to call six people, to make sure somebody else wasn't moving something else there."

Initially, designers and engineers gathered on-site every morning to plan and sketch the day's tasks, handing those instructions directly to the work crews, Richelhoff recalls. "We never could look at a set of drawings and say, 'This is what we'll be building a month from now.'"

Indeed, builders were nipping at our heels the entire half year. "We'd feed them the information exactly when they needed it," recalls interior designer Deana

MacKenzie. While intense, the hectic pace fuelled enthusiasm by making progress all the more apparent, she adds. "You could do a sketch in the office in the morning, and by afternoon go out and see it built on-site."

Client bombardment.

Having pushed this sled out of the gate, Intuit hung on with remarkable tenacity. Most clients interact only with the architect or builder, but Intuit was bombarded from all sides as issues arose: Where do you want your dining nook? How many meeting rooms? Who gets offices, and where? Can we switch flooring to shave costs?

"Fortunately, with Intuit, we had a client sophisticated enough to understand the concept of lifetime costing, but not sophisticated enough to interfere with the process. They're really good project managers, and they had the vision to know what they wanted at the end, but they're software developers; they don't know a lot about construction. If we had been working with a large developer, they'd have had their own construction group, with systems set up over 10 years. It can be a great risk for them to throw all those out the window." ~Tony Grice

Joining Controller Rodrigo on the front line, Facilities Manager Cheryll Watson fielded a good many of those panic calls. She learned firsthand the complexity of ordering items such as security hardware even before the shell was constructed. "Obviously, security is very important to us because of the information we manage," she notes. "We had to actually walk through the building in our minds to determine how we wanted particular doors to work." As a result, the folks at Intuit know more about their building than any client we've worked with. Not only do they know the price of that door hardware and where every pipe and gasket is, but they're intimately familiar with the sustainable features imbedded throughout. That knowledge should translate into long-term operational efficiency as Watson and her staff operate the facility.

As decision points arose, Intuit leaders interrupted their lives at odd hours to field urgent calls. Recalling the resulting personal chats about swimming lessons and chauffeur duty, Sims says, "Intuit bought into a process that relied heavily on their interaction with everybody. If they hadn't done that, we'd still be out there.

"You don't find very many owners that hang on as strongly to both the budget and the schedule and don't ever give up on one of them. I thought for sure Nimal (Rodrigo) would back off on one before the time was up, but he didn't on either one." ~Bill Giebelhaus

"They may not whistle while they work, but Intuit Canada's satisfied staff have helped it to place second among the 50 Best Companies To Work For In Canada....Intuit's new south Edmonton headquarters played a major role in the ranking." ~*David Finlayson*

Fast-forward construction.

The fast track that made life frenetic for our designers and difficult for Intuit put equal stress on Clark Builders. "Construction is really a sequential operation," observes Brian Robinson. "You can compress a timeline a certain amount, but you can't put the roof on before you have a foundation."

We soon learned the value of hyper-tracking with a builder whose collegial attitude has earned respect from a plethora of subtrades. "Our ability to keep pushing ahead had a lot to do with Clark's access to material and equipment," recalls McCutcheon, whose work as Manasc Isaac's project manager would have been doubly difficult otherwise. "They'd put in a call, and subtrades would do the job first, then work the paperwork out." It wasn't at all unusual for suppliers to converge on-site with samples for on-the-spot refinement, thus eliminating the restocking and delay charges that accrue when an entire order arrives, deficiencies intact. "People kept remarking they wouldn't be there if it hadn't been for Terry Richelhoff," McCutcheon adds. "They had complete trust in Terry."

As Construction Manager for Clark Builders, Richelhoff warned suppliers from the start that the compressed schedule would require everyone to "throw traditional thinking out the window." A few reality checks taught the entire team to respect that timeline. It was critical to lay the floor on schedule, for example, but everyone knew the multitude of systems running underneath would be harder to install once the floor was in place. "When trades saw the floor going down, there was a huge push to complete work under the floor. After that, I could say the schedule was the schedule. If they couldn't keep up, they would get covered up, so to speak," Richelhoff says, chuckling at the memory. "So the trades would work really hard, bringing extra crews on weekends, to make sure that didn't happen to them."

Project Superintendent Dave Wardrop and side-kick Kevin Nelson worked their own miracles on a site that swarmed with as many as 200 workers. Despite the hectic schedule and crush of people onsite, the job chalked up zero lost-time injuries, a remarkable feat in itself. Wardrop and Nelson still shake their heads about the Intuit timeline. "When I first heard, I told them they were crazy," Wardrop racalls in trademark deadpan. "I still think they're crazy, and how we did it, I don't know." But in truth, Wardrop does know. He took just one day off in those six months, and can attest to the truth behind the job start-up rules, penned by a realist back at the office: "Starting time: 7 a.m. Quitting time: When Dave says so."

Hyper tracking injected a certain efficiency into the Intuit marathon. "Quite often a single element can move around 48 times because everybody wants the perfect project," says engineer Tony Grice. "You can get into an endless loop of looking at little details and miss the big picture. But this schedule didn't allow that to happen. At each point, we had to make the right decision." Besides, he adds, "If you're plotting a drawing that somebody is waiting to drive to the site so it can be built today, it's an adrenaline rush."

"I must say that I am a neophyte when it comes to construction. So the things that I believed to be easily solvable turned out, some of them, to be very, very difficult. So yeah, absolutely, I came to appreciate the complexity of the process itself." ~Nimal Rodrigo

Designers echo that observation. "For all the tight deadlines, it felt very productive because you could measure your progress daily, recalls Sandra Valens. "Every time we'd drive out to the site, it would have grown dramatically. In retrospect, there are things we would've liked more time to contemplate, but they certainly got a lot of building for the money."

There were downsides to the pace, beyond the distinct lack of personal life for key players. Because construction began before design was complete, we had to live with decisions that, in a conventional process, would be finessed as plans evolved. Further, construction began before we knew whether the budget would bear everything we wanted to incorporate, because we didn't have complete set of documents for contractors to bid on. Educated guesses were the order of the day.

Speed also narrowed the range of feasible materials. "Your colour palette gets adjusted, because anything that's not in stock takes longer to get," notes Sims. Given that constraint, he adds, it was a godsend that Clark Builders' Richelhoff proved "a mighty fine shopper."

"When I look at that project, what I immediately think about is that the budgeting that we did and how the project came right on budget. We were able to bring it in on target, and that was done from preliminary sketches and very little information. We put it together and maintained it." ~Aftab Jessa

"Could we have done things differently? In some cases, yes," admits Owner's Agent Atan Das. Acoustics need some fine tuning, for example, and at least one meeting room is proving too small. To avoid stretching out the construction schedule, mechanical piping takes a circuitous route rather than running a direct line under that all-important floor. "But for a project this fast-paced, it's one of the best I've come across, with the fewest problems. Stretched to nine months, the design might have been better, but it would have cost more, too."

Clark Builders' Brian Robinson, by contrast, says he would hold out for a saner schedule: "I'm not sure all those pieces would ever fit together again in that same time frame." At the start, Intuit had no idea what miracles it was seeking, he notes. "If something needs to happen faster, Intuit just throws more people at it. But in construction, certain things can't happen on top of each other. In their psyche, they didn't understand."

"Intuit had a vision of what they wanted, and they're really good project managers, but they'd never built a building before. Like the rest of us, they learned a lot." *~Tony Grice*

Perhaps it's just as well Intuit didn't know, muses Yakowich, whose family has finally recovered from the shock of seeing him again. "Then they wouldn't have thought we could build it as fast. And we wouldn't have had chance to do it."

"I guess the funniest moment I had on this project was looking the builder and the contractor in the eye and telling them that we were going to be done by November. Just to see the expression on their faces."

Afterward.

"It's not over when it's over, especially when you try to do something different," says Aftab Jessa, Clark Builders' senior estimator. "You think you've covered all the bases, but there's always something minor to be fixed."

From Intuit's point of view, some of the fixes required once they'd moved in seemed anything but minor. Several resulted from the firm's rapid growth, or from planning glitches, or from the speed of construction. A few meeting rooms soon proved too small, for example, and ceiling treatment requested for aesthetic reasons didn't provide the desired level of sound proofing.

Troubleshooting deficiencies required tenacity, in part because the systems used in the Intuit building were not routine.

The annoying buzz, for example, came from fan coil units used to move hot and cold air through the underfloor gap created by the access floor. Quite large, and mounted on wood rather than the usual steel, some of those fans had shifted off-centre, and needed secure anchors. Working on the fans proved a challenge in the tight underfloor quarters, prompting our engineers to ponder using smaller fans, or perhaps even above-floor fans, in future projects.

Temperature troubles proved a puzzler, until it was discovered that some wires were reversed, so that the thermostat on the top floor was actually controlling the level below. Obvious once discovered—but amazingly difficult to troubleshoot.

Complaints about low light levels came chiefly from the floor with diagonal lighting systems, prompting electrical engineer Tony Grice to rethink that design. "The lighting wasn't as flexible as we thought it was going to be once the furniture moved in," he muses. "And of course, we didn't have time to understand where the furniture was standing until Intuit moved in."

Finding and fixing such trouble spots took time at a point when both the client and the team had hoped to call the project complete. But as Grice says, "There are two ways to achieve the perfect building. One is to design away absolutely everything that might cause problems and the other is to do the construction, identify the problems that emerge and solve those that emerge." Given the Intuit timeline, ours was by necessity the latter approach. That fact, coupled with the uniqueness of our sustainable design, expanded the scope of work required once the building began doing its job.

Beyond those fixes, we worked hard to ensure that the people operating the building know how to maximize its potential. As facilities manager, Cheryl Watson not only coordinated the entire move and liaised with us about problem areas, but gained the expertise to operate the sometimes baffling controls, computerized and otherwise. Hers is also the task of cajoling the humans inside to take ownership of the building in a way that makes it truly sustainable. The fact that she and others at Intuit know more about their building than any client we've worked with should help, translating into long-term operational efficiency.

Watson admits to some frustrations as her team made the building theirs. "Obviously there's a one-year warranty period, and it's there for a reason," she muses. "As you go through the whole first year of your occupancy, you go through the different seasons, and each season is going to have its own challenge. We've experienced some challenges, but I'm comfortable that everyone is going to meet these challenges with the same enthusiasm and drive that they did to complete the project on time."

Powered by passion.

Talk to anyone involved in the Intuit project, and you'll soon hear the word trust. "The biggest asset in this whole project was the trust that everybody had in each other, says Clark Builders' Brian Robinson. "At almost every point, work proceeded before we had complete plans or paperwork in hand. Everybody was working on sheer faith."

Without that trust, the project would have failed, says Bill Giebelhaus, Clark Builders partner and senior vice president, construction. "One of the things I preached from day one was that there would have to be a team focus for all parties. This couldn't be the normal way of doing construction; people would have to give and take in an environment like this, if we stood any chance of getting done."

Applause abounds as each partner describes how others pulled their weight. "With a tricky site and a schedule from hell, there was a lot of potential for finger pointing, but everyone was fabulous," Sims muses. "We could have fought every day. Instead, we got to know each other on a very personal level. We became one office, not three entities. With Intuit, we got fairly close, and that fosters the type of design we strive for. And the amazing thing is, we're still friends."

Owner's agent Atan Das agrees. "It was an absolute experience to be with those guys, to get it done together. The psychology and synergy were critical. And it was not as if we did any special team building effort. No, we came together because we had one objective: to build the building Intuit needed, on time. We demonstrated to a lot of people in the city and others, including the mayor, that a project like this is doable. Even Intuit's U.S. head office now believes it can be done."

"I think a few people said, 'These guys are nuts.' But we actually had fun. Most of the people probably look back on the project as a positive experience, and not as 'Oh man, my biggest nightmare in the world.' Because we became a very close knit group, nobody intentionally wanted to let anybody else down. And we're happy with the results." ~Terry Richelhoff

Intuit's attitude was critical to the mix, Giebelhaus adds. "We needed to know we had a client who was reputable, who could pay. We had to have confidence Intuit would honour what being committed to, and had willingness to do what needed to be done to get there."

As the 12-month warranty period closed, with nearly all design issues addressed, we were happy to see Intuit named Canada's second-best company to work for (Hewitt Associates/The Globe and Mail, 50 Best Companies to Work for in Canada) and to hear Intuit leaders tout their headquarters as a major player in the ranking. Most of all, we take pride in creating a signature facility, proof that a building can be attractive and tech friendly as well as energy efficient and comfortable.

Any effort that convinces more owners, contractors and subtrades to hop on the sustainable bandwagon is time well spent. As designer Deana MacKenzie says, "It's not only about the high price of energy. It's about the planet in 20 years, about our kids and grandchildren. We should've been doing this a long time ago."

" There are cycles of life, of suffering, of surviv-

al. The aboriginal view of elements or seasons or

song lines or winds may lack the energy of the

linear but it has shapes which can be tumbled

or bruised by any wave and still have mean-

ing. Our rigid frameworks simply shatter and

become a helpless part of the fragments which

shower down upon us" ~*John Ralston Saul*

Amiskwaciy

Academy

Amiskwaciy Academy: Raising the bar.

There are Cardinal Rules at Amiskwaciy Academy—non-negotiables regarding student conduct laid down by Dr. Phyllis Cardinal, the high school's principal. Since signing on with Edmonton Public Schools to create a Native-focused academy within the 208-school system, Cardinal has held fast to a rule of her own: in this school, students will not make do with second-rate.

In a move that turned traditional thinking upside down, the team behind Amiskwaciy Academy created the promised first-rate atmosphere in a second-incarnation structure, a sturdy concrete building that served for a quarter century as Edmonton's Municipal Airport terminal. Where passengers once hurried to their gates, now students study chemistry and Cree in whimsically-shaped classrooms, taking pride in a learning environment where they finally feel at home.

> "Amiskwaciy to me is a masterpiece because of the dreams that have come together to create such a beautiful place. It is really inspiring."
> ~Amiskwaciy student

"Many Aboriginal students have had an awful lot of second-hand stuff in their lives. We owe these students the very best we could muster, given what we have."~Angus McBeath

Amiskwaciy (pronounced a-MISK-wa-chee) Academy began in 1999 as a gleam in the eye of public school leaders who heeded the message behind abysmal academic scores and 75 per cent drop-out rates among Aboriginal students, and made it a priority to serve those students better. With more than 5,500 self-declared Aboriginal students in the system and the promise of expanded numbers to come, recalls now-Superintendent Angus McBeath (then in charge of schools and district services), it seemed time to apply a concept that was proving itself in numerous other programs of choice: a school tailored to the need.

"It was painstakingly put together," McBeath says of Amiskwaciy, recalling barriers met along a daunting journey from moulding philosophy to reeling in dollars to finding and fitting the right site. "But we always believed it was possible. I think that drove us to keep our eye on what it is we wanted for these young people." What they sought, he adds, was a high school that fused academic excellence with a safe, culturally rich environment. "We decided to offer the highest level of academic courses, because we wanted to counteract the notion that Aboriginal kids can't learn." Equally important were those non-negotiables regarding student conduct, made feasible by onsite support from Native Elders, career advisors, addictions counsellors and other social services. Finally, "there was this overarching piece about Aboriginal culture and spirituality. We knew that, in society, students encounter racism. We wanted them to know their traditions and beliefs, so they can become proud and strengthened in who they are."

"The government has always shunted us off into the bush with our ceremonies. We're talking hundreds of years of genocide, third and fourth generation since the time of colonization, and we've been placed in a class system where as late as 1967 we weren't allowed to vote. We need to take our rightful place."
~Phyllis Cardinal

For Phyllis Cardinal, becoming principal of this fledgling school within a mammoth 80,000-student system was itself a leap of faith—or as she terms it, "a bit of madness." Would the system be flexible enough to embrace Aboriginal perspectives rather than squeezing the new school into existing norms? "I knew it was a challenge," recalls the Saddle Lake First Nation member, who holds multiple graduate degrees and has consulted with numerous northern reserves. "A challenge for them more than for me, because my thoughts and ways of doing things are certainly unorthodox, out of the box."

Drawn to the challenge by memories of broken trust from her growing-up days in Edmonton, Cardinal's decision was confirmed as she interviewed prospective students, and found that little has changed. "One hundred per cent of them spoke about racism and discrimination and how school just didn't work for them."

The fact that dropping out remains the route of least resistance among Aboriginal teens diminishes hope not only for another generation of youth, but for Canada as a whole, Cardinal adds. At a time when government and industry leaders bemoan a shrinking pool of skilled labour, Native youth make up the fastest growing segment of western Canada's population, a bird in the hand that could, given different conditions, be instrumental in meeting tomorrow's need. "Historically, our people helped the Euro-Canadians survive on this land. With the workforce dwindling, we need to look at our young people as taking key positions—and rightfully so. That hasn't been the case, nor was the system designed for it to be."

In seeking a better way, Cardinal and her team visited programs with similar philosophies, including the Frederick Douglass Academy originally launched by Lorraine Monroe, now a beacon of hope in New York City's Harlem. While borrowing from those initiatives, she built an Edmonton solution by consulting Aboriginal parents and seeking the advice of Native Elders.

"We wanted to challenge the stereotypes, I think, both Phyllis and me. You've got to demonstrate that these young people are capable of learning and participating in society. It's absolutely crucial to demonstrate that, so it becomes more pervasively believed."
~Angus McBeath

Those Elders envisioned a school that combines ancient wisdom—including an emphasis on Mother Earth, sacred colours, seasonal change, circular reality and the four compass points—with training in 21st century skills. They also gave the school its name, a shortened form of the Cree word for early Edmonton: Amiskwaciy Waskahegan (Beaver Hills House). And they offered three guiding principles: collaboration, vision and no blame.

Such groundings unite everyone at Amiskwaciy in a deep sense of accountability, Cardinal says. "In our natural law, we are given responsibility as children and as young people and as adults and as elders in the community to honour and respect our roles and responsibility." For students here, that means striving for an 80 percent academic average—and religiously following those Cardinal Rules.

Amiskwaciy Project Timeline

Summer 1999:
Edmonton Public School Board commits to an Aboriginal high school

January 2000:
Client workshops and site search begin

Spring 2000:
Vacant air terminal chosen as preferred long-term site, subject to rezoning and lease negotiations

June 2000:
Alberta Learning commits $12 million in innovation funding to Amiskwaciy Academy

September 2000:
Temporary site opens while work on permanent home continues

February 2002:
Renovations complete at 101 Airport Road and students move in

June 2002:
Official opening ceremonies, with Governor General Adrienne Clarkson participating

November 2002:
Gymnasium and interior sweat lodge complete

Amisckwaciy Academy:
A Runway for High Flyers

Unable to pry capital dollars for a new building from provincial coffers, loath to put an out-of-the-box program in a traditional school building, Edmonton Public Schools adopted a tactic in launching Amiskwaciy Academy that has proven successful in other innovative programs: leasing an existing structure rather than constructing and owning a new facility. For Manasc Isaac Architects, that decision opened the door to an instructive case study in the sustainability of adaptive reuse.

Finding exactly the right place to offer Aboriginal students respectful education proved a journey in itself. Leading the search was realtor Mark Kolke, who had helped negotiate leases for Edmonton Public's Centre High (for students needing more than three years to finish high school) and Metro Community College (for lifelong learning). Based on those experiences, Edmonton Public Schools' Brian Fedor called us in to help determine Amiskwaciy's space needs with Principal Phyllis Cardinal, with whom we'd worked in Saddle Lake.

"The Aboriginal community was looking for a unique location. Number one, they wanted a place they could truly create as their own and not impact or be impacted by neighbouring area. They were very much against a traditional school setting."~Roland Labbe

Upon joining the team, we launched directly into the client workshops for which we've become known. Because neither teaching staff nor students were yet identified, we couldn't include those crucial groups at this stage, but we did pull in school district program planners and Aboriginal liaison experts. Their insights, together with the strong vision provided by Cardinal and Edmonton Public School's Angus McBeath, gave us rich fodder for both a feasibility plan and site selection concepts.

Indeed, those leaders posed specific and strongly held criteria. "It had to be a building with lots of space for both gathering and classroom learning, lots of flexibility, but also one that looked first class," McBeath recalls, "because a building says something about what we believe in you." To minimize both temptation and conflict, the list of forbidden neighbours included shopping malls and existing high schools as well as residential areas that might prove less than welcoming. Among desired traits were good transit connections, eastern exposure, natural light, green space and outdoor teaching areas. Oh yes, and we needed as much as 90,000 square feet, a large footprint.

"Strengthening Aboriginal learner success is important to all Albertans." ~Lyle Oberg

Those criteria in hand, Kolke recalls, "We cast our net wide with design concepts. The team quickly winnowed the choices down to eleven finalists. We had seen all but one option by the time we pulled up at the empty air terminal." The 86,443-square-foot facility proved an instant winner with Amiskwaciy's principal, Kolke recalls. "Phyllis walked around and said, 'This is it.'"

"We couldn't have afforded to build a building that size. We knew we would never have the resources. And none of our closed schools would have met all of our criteria." ~Angus McBeath

Indeed, the building lends itself well to use as an alternative high school, says Public School planner Roland Labbe. "It is high quality institutional construction, which provided significant savings. It's quite roomy, with high ceilings, and it offered many opportunities to create very unique spaces." Equally important, it fulfilled the First Nations desire to make a clean break with bad memories. "Because the airport had not been a school before, they were comfortable with the location." More central than most other options, yet ten minutes away from downtown, it is well-served by public transit. Rather than belonging to (or being seen to invade) any one neighbourhood, it belongs to the city as a whole.

Richard Isaac: The workshops weren't as extensive as they normally are for us, because there were very few staff and no pupils. That did lead to problems later on. I had to then do that work with people individually. Vivian Manasc: Which actually is an interesting observation on the workshop process itself. That if you do it at the beginning, you save yourself a lot of work later

As an added benefit, Labbe adds, "the Aboriginal community was fairly familiar and comfortable with the airport itself, since that terminal has served many of their northern communities a great deal over the years. So there was almost a natural identity and attachment there. Because of those strong aviation ties, the school is very interested in pursuing relations with aviators and the aviation industry." Although the passenger terminal has been closed since 1996, when Edmonton City Council consolidated scheduled passenger travel at the Edmonton International Airport, the adjacent runway continues to serve Canada's second most active general aviation airport. Before long, however, a combination of funding and zoning issues made it clear that facility would not be ready for Amiskwaciy's intended September 2000 opening. To avoid losing momentum, school administrators decided to find a temporary location.

This threw another ball into our court. Already hyper-tracking Intuit headquarters, we now carved a chunk out of the summer to fit up a downtown site known as the R.H. David Building as an interim home for the 290 students who enrolled in Amiskwaciy that first September. Fortunately, the site's previous incarnation as a telecommunications training facility, coupled with the fact that it sat within hailing distance of our offices, made that project less complex than it might have been.

Meanwhile, in the typical rollercoaster fashion that keeps architecture interesting, we'd received both good news and bad. On the up side, Alberta Learning announced in June that it would fund Amiskwaciy to the tune of $2 million a year for six years as a pilot program. The money would have to stretch across both capital and operating expenses, mind you, still ruling out new construction, but it would allow us to lease a building if the landlord agreed to foot good chunks of the renovations. Some federal heritage dollars also were flowing in to support Native Elders' presence in the school, after considerable jockeying about which level of government was responsible for what. And a trickle of corporations, including Bank of Montreal and EPCOR, offered support.

On the down side, the very heritage that added value to the terminal from the Aboriginal perspective was raising ghosts of airport battles past. For the people who opposed amalgamating the airports, putting that building into some other use was its death knell as a terminal.

Determined to address those concerns, we proposed to separate students from the airport tarmac with a double barrier of industrial fencing fronted by berms. Taxiing giant Hercules past the building, we found the structure remarkably sound resistant, but made plans to up the comfort level in strategic spots. With the promise of lights and action in a facility that deserved a new lease on life as certainly as the students destined to use it, City Council approved rezoning to accommodate the school.

Approval in hand, Edmonton Public Schools negotiated an agreement with building owner Gibralt Capital Corporation that funded a good chunk of the renovations through landlord lease incentive. Striking that deal and using that building not only allowed the district to meet an urgent need but reaped significant savings, Labbe says. "I would think we saved more than 50 per cent on the building side, over what we would have spent to start from scratch. And that excludes land costs, because we're just leasing. It's a direction we've chosen to go in this environment, where we've not been successful in receiving traditional capital support, and we've met with pretty good success so far."

"Mitigating noise is one of the challenges of sustainable design; in this case we focused on it because we had to demonstrate that this would be a quiet and healthy environment. It was a reasonable request, to make sure it was no noisier than other schools."

"We had acoustic consultants measure

and predict noise,

levels throughout the school. All areas

are well within accepted acoustic levels

for classrooms"

"Our acoustical studies demonstrated that

NOISE

in classrooms is simply a non-issue.

In a few areas, we recommended

increased glazing of windows, but

when you're inside, noise is not a factor."

~Roland Labbe

Flying through time.

Edmonton City Centre Airport began life in the mid-1920s, named Blatchford Field after then-Mayor Ken Blatchford. It became part of the federal government's Second World War effort from 1939 to 1945, was renamed the Edmonton Industrial Airport in 1963 and Edmonton Municipal Airport (The Muni) in 1975. In 1975 the air terminal building was designed by Groves Hodgson Architects, as a wide open commuter airport terminal. With increasing security reqirements the building was renovated over the course of the next 20 years. The site came under the Edmonton Regional Airports Authority umbrella in 1996 following rigorous debate that culminated in a plebiscite. With most scheduled passenger traffic consolidated south of the city at the Edmonton International Airport in a bid to attract more direct flights, the 1970s-built downtown terminal building stood empty for half a decade before becoming home to Amiskwaciy Academy.

Green space.

For our landscape team, the fact that Amiskwaciy sits in an aviation zone raised not only expectations but challenges, beginning immediately behind the back door where jets previously taxied up. "The airside tarmac is a metre or more thick," explains David Brown of Gibbs & Brown, who tackled the challenge of turning tarmac green. "That became a big problem, because it limited our ability to provide at-grade landscaping."

Instead, Brown incorporated raised berms between the school and the all-important security fence. Originally conceived as sweetgrass islands with an eagle feather motif, those berms stretched lengthwise when sound became an issue. Sloped to taller than human height at the back, widening to eight metres as they near the fence, the berms do an admirable job of buffering sound, particularly at ground level where the building has less inbuilt noise control. The upper floor, where passengers once waited, already had the insulation and glazing needed to muffle runway noise.

"Noise is not an issue at all. The berms are a sound and visual barrier, and on the second floor, the teachers keep their blinds open or not, depending on their teaching style. I don't think it's a bad thing when students can visually see the planes take off. It's a sort of window to the rest of the world."~Shirly McNeill

Besides serving as a noise attenuation wall, the fan-shaped berms accomplish their aesthetic purpose. No longer bare tarmac, the space behind the school now feels inviting, its berms appropriately angled to the sky. As Brown says, "They have quite a visual impact for those flying in and out of the Muni."

The berms also offer the potential for outdoor learning. Each contains traditional vegetation related by use: in the first, you'll find common household aids; in the second, medicinal remedies; in the third, ceremonial ingredients. "We chose native plantings that correspond with the school curriculum," Brown says. "Hopefully in future this will provide a really unique program space for staff and students."

Amid thousands of shoots installed during a student plantathon, an abundance of weeds sprouted that first summer, intruders likely carted in with the topsoil. Once these native species are established, though, they will prove hardy as well as educationally useful, Brown predicts. A sustainable strategy even at an airport, native plant materials have the best chance of survival. Careful design also ensures they receive enough rain from natural sources, mitigating the need for sprinklers.

Because buildings tend to settle over time, drainage issues often crop up on established sites. The surrounding tarmac made it harder to correct those issues here, Brown says. "We tried to channel water away from the school, under the berms and onto the airstrip. But even now, there's a bit of ponding between the school and the berm walls because there's minimal grade back there."

Life in a flight zone also comes with regulations about allowable plant species. "First of all, we had lots of limitations in regard to planting trees due to height restrictions," Brown recalls. "And we couldn't plant species of shrubs that had berries, because they might attract birds and wildlife. We went through a lot of review on those items."

A mid-course decision to build a gym west of the school added new wrinkles to the landscape puzzle. While an important component, particularly because the nearest outdoor playing fields are a jog away, the gym consumed a fair chunk of the minimal space available for landscaping. After initial footings were laid, budget constraints forced the gym to shrink, returning a chunk of the outdoors to our landscape team with a new challenge: orphaned footings. As construction on the gym and related items inside the school (including locker rooms and an interior sweat lodge) continued into the fall of 2002, Brown pondered solutions ranging from a small outdoor seating area to a corn garden, intent on making the most out of the space despite a limited budget.

Indeed, this entire landscape design is characterized by making the most with little. Bounded by aviation regulations, working with limited space, Brown used bold strokes to unite the site and create inviting outdoor gathering spots. Shapes and colours echo sacred motifs chosen for the building's interior, including the school's circular, four-pointed logo. A sodded centre island, for example, recalls the tradition of the sacred circle. Along the building's front, red metal benches echo rails and arrow-like scaffolding around a second-floor balcony. As Brown observes, "We provided just enough to make an impact and provide some functionality."

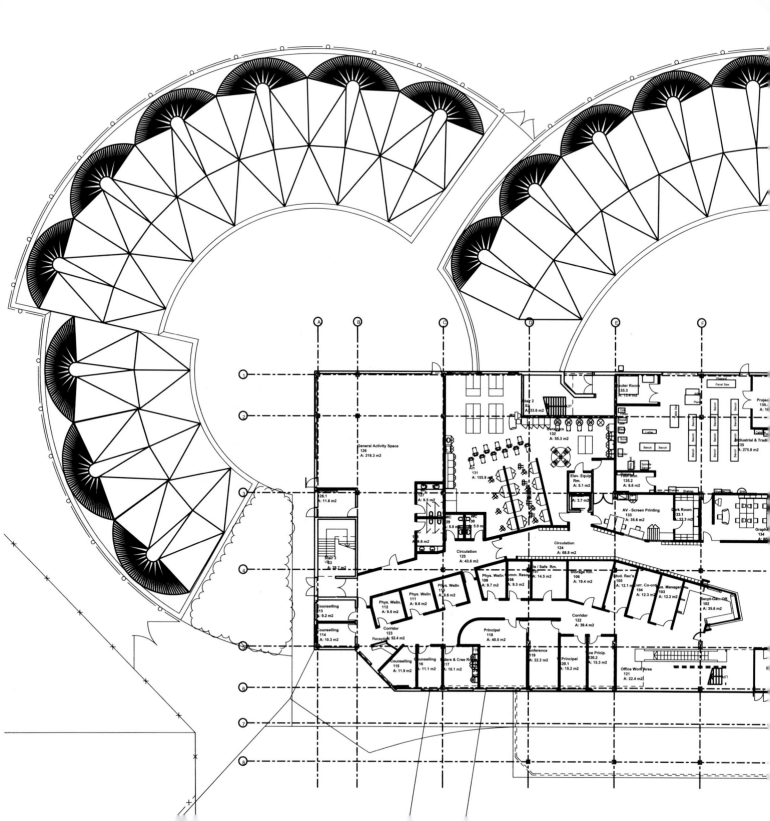

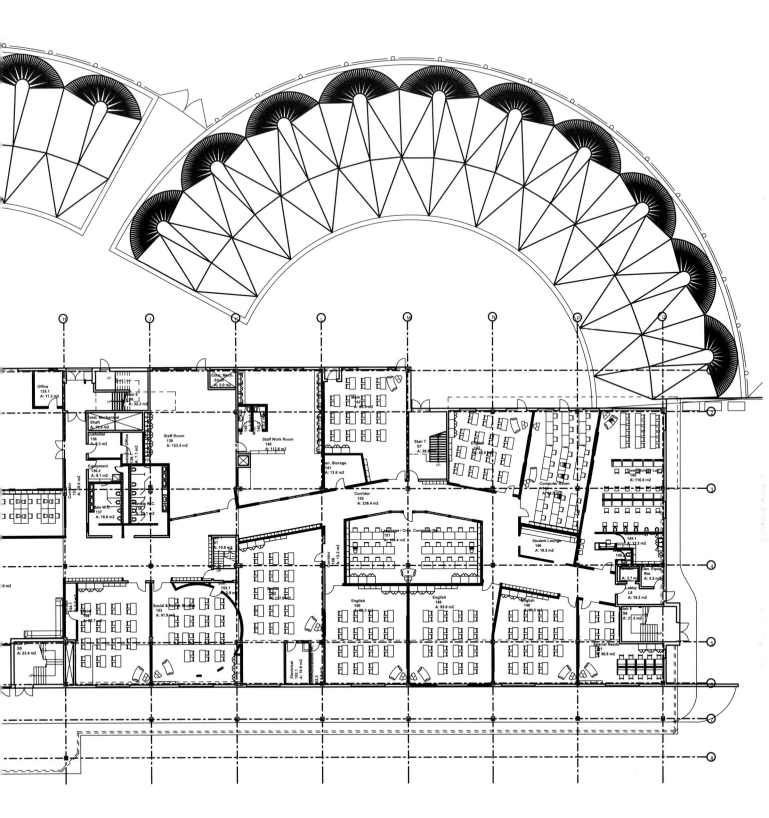

Constructing the vision.

One of the first steps in turning the airport terminal into a high school, ironically, involved undoing some of our own previous work. We'd designed various renovations in the building's earlier incarnation, including a security wall that essentially cut the space in half lengthwise, truncating interior sightlines. Partner Richard Isaac, who provided design direction for the Amiskwaciy project, recalls the demolition of that wall as a particularly satisfying moment.

But before the wall came down—indeed, before renovation began—we invited key team members to a half-day partnering workshop where we as architects and engineers described the intent behind our design, and invited response. "All the major subcontractors came out," recalls Jack Jones, whose Cavan Contractors Ltd. managed the job. "More than anything, it brought in some ownership from everyone involved."

"Unlike the Intuit project, where we bridged the gap at the beginning because everybody started at the same time, this project followed a more conventional model in which the design team starts first and the construction team gets plugged in. The partnering workshop is really the opportunity to give the story that goes with the construction documents. The intent is to reduce the adversarial nature of the construction process by making sure that both teams are on the same page."

To their credit, public school leaders specifically requested the workshop; just five years earlier, pulling the entire team together beforehand to make sure we're on the same page had been a new concept for this client. Fingering the thick stack of Amiskwaciy design specifications that was his bible during this project, intern architect Shafraaz Kaba contemplates the reasons why partnering workshops win converts. "Many subcontractors are given just one sheet of this whole package. When they're focused on just that little tiny thing, they'll only do it like it's shown, the quickest, fastest way. But when they have a stake in the whole thing, they ask questions that make it better, because they have a will to make it conform to the greater idea."

Design integration.

Rather than serving one community, this school intends to reflect a whole spectrum of Aboriginal cultures: Cree, Dene, Métis, Saulteaux and more. Further, because it is truly a school of choice, it must provide a sense of welcome to students of any culture. The design we shaped and then entrusted to construction crews reflects what we heard during numerous client workshops, as those closest to the project helped us translate that idea into colours, patterns and shapes.

"They really wanted to have the four colours of the medicine wheel and the primary shapes idea of general First Nations culture, without being specific to any particular one," Kaba recalls. "We gave it a twist by skewing the shapes, making ovals rather than pure circles, parallelograms rather than rectangles." The results are particularly apparent in the hallway floors, where playful geometric patterns in blue, yellow, red and aqua are cut into the linoleum, a visual feast that can also be enjoyed at a deeper level. Cardinal specifically asked that patterns down the administrative hallway, for example, depict direction and forward motion.

"With the red hand rails, what I was doing was to give some idea, some impression, of drying racks. I didn't want it too literal. Somebody said was a real good exercise in showing how you could connect rods together using the scaffold pole connections. That's fine, I much prefer people to see it however they want to. If you hit them over the head with a sledgehammer and you put a teepee on there, then that's all it can be." ~Richard Isaac

Cutting those designs into the linoleum took more than a little patience, Cavan site superintendent Marlin Johnson wryly observes. "We thought a few of those fellas might have to end up in some kind of institute." But the finished floor sets the intended tone from the moment a person enters the reincarnated building and walks across a huge sunny circle bursting with ribbons of red. "The way it was handled was great," enthuses Cavan's Jones. "In a lot of the jobs we've done, the architect will put a lot of patterning in a classroom. It looks great until you put in all the desks, and then you lose it all. But here, it was used in the corridors and main foyer, the high traffic flow areas."

"The problem I've had sometimes with First Nations projects is the apparent desire to be too literal in terms of the interpretation of nativism. Of course the modern day Native has connections with teepees and canoes, but I think that a lot of them, especially the younger ones, really would like somewhat more modern interpretations. Phyllis isn't too keen on literal either. So I think we were quite successful here." ~*Richard Isaac*

In many ways, the fact that we were working with an existing building—and a well-built one at that—simplified our design task. As Isaac notes, we had numerous givens, many of them beneficial or at least benign: sturdy concrete construction, traffic-worthy staircases and exits, large banks of solar-friendly windows. Even the building's orientation was a plus, with most large windows facing north toward the tarmac, where they don't cause excessive heat gain. We were able to retain the entire fabric of the building, from walls to washrooms, from stairs to elevator. As a bonus, the garage-like baggage handling rooms adapted particularly well to industrial arts space.

Then there were those aspects that seemed problematic, but ultimately set the stage for innovative design. Most significantly, the building is fatter than required for the usual school, whose dimensions include a middle corridor plus classrooms and offices on either side. Dealt a wider floorplate, Isaac explains, "we had to come up with a way to zigzag the corridors to connect with the exits."

The resulting dynamic adds interest not only to the hallways, but in the irregularly shaped learning spaces. "On the second floor, there are a lot of classrooms that make me wish I was a high school student again," muses Kaba lusting after a seat overlooking the runway to the north, or the downtown skyline to the south. "They're very vibrant, not your typical rectangular box."

In many classrooms, partial-ceilings appear to float in space, soaking up noise while softening the look of exposed masonry and ductwork. Like the patterned floors, those whimsically shaped "Tectum Clouds" create a design statement that attracts praise even from the crews who sweated over their installation. Taking integration a step further, engineer Tony Grice strategically placed lighting to bounce off the clouds, creating the indirect illumination that reduces eyestrain.

Hearing a clear call for meaningful gathering spaces, we opened an expansive ceremonial area on the second floor. As Kaba notes, that space boasts "a big wow value." High-ceilinged, airy and bright, it has already proven itself during such celebrations as Amiskwaciy's June 2002 official opening. The area serves double duty as an eatery, complete with an industrial kitchen that will eventually facilitate on-the-job learning. Original windows facing the tarmac, coupled with new windows cut into the north wall, eliminate the need for artificial light during large parts of the day.

Directly off the ceremonial area is an outdoor balcony rimmed by red hand rails that is proving a favourite among students. Happily facing south, this "found" space took shape in an inspired moment, when our designers realized that the overhang sheltering the downstairs doorway offered a perfect platform for those on the second floor to catch a breath of fresh air. So we cut a doorway through, opening the upstairs to the outdoors in a way that makes particular sense on a site with limited green space.

We also cut new windows into classrooms and offices on the ground floor. When concern arose that our preferred crank-out openers could obstruct pedestrians on sidewalks that march right up to the building, we used small louvers to introduce fresh air. Our choice of materials also paid heed to indoor air quality. Linoleum won out over carpet, for example, because even environmentally friendly carpet harbours dirt and germs when subjected to the abuse of a school setting

Concerned to minimize waste, we found homes for as many interior fittings as possible. In some cases, the result was clearly advantageous. Industrial kitchen equipment salvaged from two former airport cafeterias not only equipped Amiskwaciy's cafeteria, but created a domestic science room that's a cut above the norm. Similarly, it's not every school that has its own emergency generator or air conditioning, two holdovers from the previous incarnation that ideally won't be used much, but are available if needed.

Retaining the main boiler plant was more of a mixed blessing, Isaac notes. "It was a balancing act between tearing it out and scrapping it, or leaving it with its inbuilt inefficiencies." In the end, both the boiler and the air handling system were upgraded and used with new circuitry and ductwork. We also added vestibules to maximize comfort and minimize energy loss.

The fact that the building was designed to run such energy-hungry devices as luggage conveyor belts also had its downsides, notes engineer Tony Grice. "We had all this power available to us, but these huge transformers sitting in the basement can generate a lot of heat. So we actually changed the configuration of some of that equipment, just to get rid of those inefficiencies."

Amiskwaciy – sustainable strategies.

Site:
- Well-located, near existing bus routes, the school is well-served by public transportation
- Parking was not increased; existing parking was more than adequate for the school.
- The school is designed to accommodate students arriving by bicycle, and showers are provided.
- Site planting was increased, without the use of irrigation, by planting berms with native plant species

Water:
- No irrigation added to the site. Existing storm-water systems were sufficient to accommodate expanded building capacity.
- No increase in plumbing fixtures. Most existing plumbing fixtures retained.

Energy:
- Energy consumption decreased by the re-use and modification of existing boilers and power distribution systems.
- Although the building envelope was not modified, the reduced demand and reduced building systems result in reductions in energy use.
- Direct/indirect lighting in classrooms reduces power consumption and improves visual environment.

Materials:
- Recyclables are collected at the school, as part of the overall approach of Edmonton Public Schools.
- 100% of the building structure and shell were re-used.
- Of the non-shell elements, all washrooms were re-used, as were the bulk of the building systems.
- A construction waste management plan was specified.
- Rapidly-renewable materials such as linoleum were used on most of the floor surfaces.

Environmental Quality:
- Acoustics were improved with the addition of berms between air traffic and educational spaces.
- Indoor Air quality was designed to current standards, with increased ventilation effectiveness integrated into mechanical systems design.
- Low-emitting materials and sealants were specified through-out the school.
- Operable windows were added on the ground-side of the building.
- All classrooms have daylight and access to views is provided from all offices, workshops and classrooms.
- Sound quality in the classrooms is carefully monitored.
- Thermal mass left exposed, by using suspended "clouds" for acoustical absorption.

Innovation:
- Leasing rather that construction a school was an innovative strategy for educational facility development.
- Culturally-specific educational facilities in an urban setting support evolving sustainable communities.
- Re-use of a vacant building for community use improves urban density.

The plethora of conduit did open the door to reuse of lighting hardware, Grice added. "We changed all the fixtures because nothing was suitable, but we very carefully went through how the existing lighting was set up in terms of switching and circuits, and designed a lighting system to accommodate the existing infrastructure."

The building's solid construction became less of an asset when new lines needed to be run, Jones recalls. "When you're cutting through that concrete to change plumbing lines, it's quite a task." On the other hand, that sturdy character inspired imitation, he adds. "That building is going to be there a long time, so we tried to introduce products that have that same durability as well."

In every project, the inevitable crunch of dollars and time leaves each of us with a personal regret or two. Shafraaz Kaba would have taken the extra time to leave more original masonry exposed; Isaac regrets not having the budget to improve a building envelope that, typical of its period, is less than ideal.

Amiskwaciy administrators proved essential in sorting must-haves from like-to-haves, Jones recalls. "In some cases, things we may think are important are not to them. There were also some areas where we could reuse materials from the existing campus—lockers, for example, and some of the whiteboards. It's important to have that input from users."

We would have loved to give Amiskwaciy an energy-saving down-filled parka like Hinton's. But the fact remains that, by not building a new structure, Amiskwaciy has already saved more energy than this building will consume in many decades. A new 90,000-square-foot school would have required at least 5000 tons of materials; using an existing building saved the extraction and erection of all those materials. In terms of lifecycle savings, this project succeeded even before the first students walked through those doors on Feb. 24, 2002.

Open for learning.

Because Amiskwaciy Academy is a school, the ultimate proof of its success is in the learning. Indeed, learning seems contagious among the 350 students who moved here in February 2002, as evidenced by steadily improving marks and a drop-out rate of zero.

"Many of our students have not had success in school," observes Vice Principal Shirly McNeill. "Here, there's the expectation that you're going to strive for 80 per cent, that you shouldn't expect any less. With opportunity and support, you can see students becoming quite delighted with themselves as scholars." She recalls the student who, when congratulated on her skyrocketing marks, responded, "Yeah, and next year, I'm going to rock." It's a self-fulfilling prophecy that, for once, is spiraling up rather than down.

True, the building cannot take credit for miracles accomplished by the people inside, from principal to cook, Elder to janitor. Yet there's no doubt the environment itself is part of the team, enabling the school's emerging spirit. "It's such a beautiful space," McNeill muses. The abundant windows in the classrooms invite connections not only with the outdoors, but with life in the hallways, speaking volumes about the open, collaborative learning modeled here. "As you move through the building, you can see the learning happening."

Students come here from as far away as Labrador, Northwest Territories and Saskatchewan as well as all across Alberta, often drawn by word of mouth. Despite the plethora of nations represented, "there are no issues among the kids related to band or affiliation," McBeath says. "Those issues do exist in the adult community, but this is a very pan-Aboriginal school. That was certainly part of our design, but we couldn't predict how it would develop."

"At first, when I heard the idea of an Aboriginal high school in this city, I didn't think it would work. I thought it would be another school of conflict and trouble. But no, not this school. Every day, when I come to school, I'm happy. Happy to be a part of this family." ~*Nicole Sharphead*

Aboriginal spirituality permeates the school, from the sweet-grass ceremonies every morning to the expectation that each student will take Cree, Native dance or Aboriginal studies. Half the staff is Aboriginal while the remainder, from a mix of cultural backgrounds, are trained in First Nation ways. Elders regularly visit classrooms, adding cultural perspectives.

"I was looking for a design that would be arresting, that would reflect Aboriginal people, that would fit our fiscal requirements and that would invite optimal teaching and learning." ~Angus McBeath "The building offered us the opportunity to create the kinds of spaces that would be in keeping with their traditions, things they wanted to introduce to students who might not be exposed to customs and practices as they might in a smaller community. It has proven to be a wonderful choice, from many perspectives." ~Roland Labbe "One of challenges in any existing building reuse is that you're dealing with the orientation you're given. But in this case, it was actually oriented relatively well. The big windows are all on the north side, so we didn't have excessive heat gain." ~Vivian Manasc "That building has huge windows that any school would die for, set up as viewing ports for the runway area. With floor-to-ceiling windows, they've got all sorts of daylight coming in." ~Tony Grice "It was just such a neat fit, to take these really robust baggage handling rooms, basically big garages, and see how they adapted really nicely for all the industrial arts you have in a high school." ~Vivian Manasc "We gave them a very nice facility, and it preserves a bit of the historical use." ~Jack Jones "I love the ceilings. I have to admit I was a little skeptical. But it's kind of a unique feature that you don't see very often, a bit of a focal point people notice when they go in." ~Jack Jones

"We integrated the lighting into the clouds so the whole thing became one element. It suited the student population; they're not traditional students, so we wanted to give them nontraditional space." ~Tony Grice "Sometimes from economic point of view it makes a lot of sense to go in with a demolition contract and strip everything out—you end up with a huge pile of garbage, but it's easier for everybody. If you're doing sustainable design, though, easy isn't always the good answer." ~Tony Grice "In a new building, we would have chance to put in opening windows and a high performing building envelope. But here, we have to adapt to what's there." ~Tony Grice "It was a great working relationship. We got to know each other very well as friends as well as just through the work. That was a nice side benefit to the project." ~Jack Jones "We've worked with Manasc Isaac for years on many different types of projects, and the other consultants on the team as well. The only reason groups turn back to each other to seek assistance is based on the commitment, knowledge and experience shown on past projects." ~David Brown "This is an excellent example of what you can do with a building that has been built to last a long time and then becomes redundant within a city like this. You can make it so functional, the way it is right now, to totally different occupancy. As you walk through the school, it shows what can be done with a building right in heart of the city." ~Bill Temple

Ceremonies play an equally important role in happier times, including the grand opening of Amiskwaciy's new home and unveiling of a grand Dale Auger mural gracing its lobby. "Last year, I couldn't believe how many ceremonies we had," muses Principal Phyllis Cardinal. "They were very powerful and very meaningful, and I believe our kids gained leaps and bounds by them." Recalling how students familiar with Native traditions guided their peers, she added, "It sure grabbed my heartstrings when I saw them. They conducted themselves in a way that many adults can't."

"Being in an environment where there are a large number of students with Aboriginal background who are very spiritual, there's a collective something—a spirit I haven't been able to find the word for—that's very nice to be around." *~Shirly McNeill*

Under scrutiny.

Amiskwaciy Academy lives under the microscope. Grade 11 student Kelly Paul is pulled out of class so often to serve as tour guide for the steady parade of visitors that he's thinking it's time to train a few friends. Beyond inquiries from school districts such as Saskatoon and Yellowknife, beyond invitations to participate in Alberta-wide consultations, national initiatives see Amiskwaciy as a model worth watching in the drive to boost achievement among First Nations youth. In fall 2001, when the National Aboriginal Achievement Foundation held Taking Pulse, an educational think tank with key corporate leaders, Amiskwaciy was prominent among the case studies and Cardinal was at the table.

"Amiskwaciy Academy... will be worth watching in the next year or two for student and teacher retention." *~ National Aboriginal Achievement Foundation*

Of course there are skeptics, including those still haunted by ghosts of segregated schools past. But as Cardinal emphasizes, "We're not a segregated school; we're a school of choice." Students apply by writing a letter of intent and obtaining letters of reference, and are admitted following an interview. A few non-Aboriginal students attend, adding a welcome dimension to the culture of the school.

The academy could accept another 400 students, more than doubling in size. "I'm sure some students are waiting until it's no longer new," McBeath says, "and it may not be for every kid. People don't go to that school who are indifferent about their culture or who don't want to learn about it, because there's no way of avoiding spirituality and Aboriginal culture there." But for some, it is an answer worth traveling long distances for, whether that means uprooting from family in the far north or, like tour guide Kelly Paul, riding transit three hours a day.

"There's a judicious blend of spirituality and culture, coupled with quite relentless expectations for student achievement and student behaviour. The power of that combination is somewhat unique." ~Angus McBeath

Amid the inevitable busyness at the leading edge, the school continues to scramble for the resources that make this place special—the people and programs that enable students to work through issues ranging from discrimination to poverty, inadequate literacy to addictive homes. With the throes of opening and then relocating finally behind, they're also putting energy into finding hosts for mentorships and apprenticeships. "Ultimately, our goal is that all of our students will have experience in the world of work, so they have this place of support as they venture out and come back," says Vice-Principal McNeill.

"If we are to make a difference, we need to make an investment in these young people. I'm just starting to take that message out to donors." ~Phyllis Cardinal

"Our biggest worry is always funding," Cardinal adds. "It's a huge concern for us, because this doesn't come without a price." But as she points out when knocking on donor doors, "The rewards will be there as our students make a difference in their own community—not as part of a penal institutions, not as a tax burden, but actually helping Canadian society. That's my vision and that's what I perceive."

Being Amiskwaciy is not easy, McBeath muses. "Maybe it never will be, for a long time." Not easy, perhaps, but essential, and a joy to behold. "I love the feeling that you get when you go there. I love watching the students and the teachers, deeply engaged in learning." Were he to spin the clock back to that time when Amiskwaciy was but a gleam in the eye, McBeath adds, "I wouldn't have done anything differently. Maybe I'd have done it sooner."

Good bones.

Just as Amiskwaciy's program offers one model for serving Aboriginal youth, so its building illustrates one viable approach to sustainable architecture. Unlike Europe, where buildings hundreds and even thousands of years old are routinely reused, Canada's west is still more apt to tear down and build anew—or simply tear down to reduce taxes and gain parking lot income, a telling statement of the worth we place in "used" buildings.

That throwaway orientation will shift, predicts architect Derek Heslop, a partner in Manasc Isaac Architects. "As our population increases and our needs change, we will, I think, be looking more and more to reusing what we already have." The air terminal was an especially fine candidate for reuse. "It was very robust, with good bones," Heslop notes, pointing to the large floor areas, few bearing walls and high ceilings. "For flexibility in using the space for other purposes than it was originally intended, that's a helpful thing."

"The most miserable buildings are so tightly fit to a program that the minute you change the use, the building becomes functionally obsolete. Ultimately one of the real lessons—and the airport is an excellent example of that—is that the more flexibly a building is designed, the least programmatically driven it is, ultimately the better for the long term."

It's a reality that has struck home for both Heslop and me as we conduct building evaluations for various clients, gaining a comparative overview of numerous health centres, schools and civic structures. Almost inevitably, the most successful of those buildings over the long term—that is, the most sustainable—are flexibly designed rather than being tightly fit to a particular use. In the 21st century whir of accelerated change, attention to that reality at every stage of a building's life has great potential to reduce the monumental waste that occurs when buildings become (or are considered) obsolete.

Capitalizing on the air terminal's flexible design, we were able to fundamentally change the building's use while retaining its essential integrity. Unlike the numerous school renovations we have known, this design took a step beyond reuse, to that horizon—opening world of adaptive reuse. Besides slicing the construction bill in half, adaptive reuse minimized environmental cost by creating far less waste and requiring fewer new materials.

For Edmonton Public Schools, as for so many urban school districts, adaptive reuse offers a potential solution to a growing conundrum—a mismatch between available schools and student needs. In the case of Amiskwaciy, that mismatch was cultural; in many instances, it's geographic. As the population shifts outward, new suburbs cry for neighbourhood schools while facilities at the core sit empty.

Mastering the mismatch requires stepping back a pace to address not only empty schools, but a community's entire spectrum of underutilized space. Only as downtown warehouses, parking lots, office towers—perhaps even schools—are adapted to affordable residential use will nearby schools refill as well. As that example suggests, viewing existing buildings through sustainability spectacles reveals useful solutions to crucial urban design and community development issues.

Amiskwaciy Academy offers a case in point. Besides meeting an urgent educational need in a central spot where no high school existed, the academy injects new life into a building that sat vacant too long, preserving those good bones for another generation to enjoy.

"With its grounding in nature, Wabi-sabi appreciates that nothing is permanent, perfect or complete. Instead, it sees beauty in the process and cycle of change and becoming. It sees perfection in imperfection, wisdom in not knowing, essence in the hidden or diminished."

~Tom Wujec, Sandra Muscat

"Before any Old Order of Things can be given the final heave-ho coup de grâce, it's necessary to create a parallel infra-structure controlled by people acting in cooperation for their own benefit and mutual support." ~Christopher Locke

"Orville Wright did not have a pilot's license."

Gordon MacKenzie

"'Journeys to relive your past?' was the Khan's question at this point, a question which could also have been formulated: 'Journeys to recover your future?'"

~*Italo Calvino*

Curiosity going forward.

Banff. Hinton. Intuit. Amiskwaciy. Say those words in our office, and four distinct buildings holograph into view. Because they mark our first steps into sustainable architecture, those projects hold particular significance, here at Manasc Isaac. We like to think they are significant, harbingers of a northern light—a light that will one day permeate the landscape. Already, a growing number of enlightened architects could tell similar tales of journeys taken and lessons learned.

Chief among those lessons: it can be done. Already, clients in sustainable buildings are enjoying up to double the savings, whether measured in kilowatts, megawatts, greenhouse gas emissions, productivity, comfort or longevity. By 2050, perhaps even before, citizens will expect new structures to be neutral to their environment, or even regenerative. Electrical and mechanical systems, where present, will be minuscule and powered onsite by natural forces such as solar and wind. Far from paying energy bills, many owners will benefit as their buildings share excess energy with the larger grid.

Our own journey into sustainability has taken surprising twists. Like many, we began by zeroing in on energy efficiency. But buildings are first and foremost for human occupancy and comfort. So sustainable design became a conversation about healthy, energy-efficient buildings—and then expanded again to encompass environmental as well as human health.

"We're at a crossroads. We can either keep going big—big dogs eat first—or take a look at distributed technology. Perhaps the grid system will no longer exist, in 2030; a lot of energy is wasted in the typical bulk power distribution system. Or maybe we connect to the grid, but in a restorative process—not as consumer, but supplier." *~Tony Grice*

The impact of waste generated during building construction and de-construction hadn't occurred to me until we were asked by Alberta Environment to study the question of construction waste. As we conducted interviews in best practice-communities across North America, it became clear that architects could have a huge impact on landfill waste by specifying different demolition and construction practices—and that some of those approaches are more effective than others. Alberta Environment had not contemplated asking architects to change their specifications, but within two years that became a key prong in the push to divert construction waste from landfill sites. Meanwhile, we've integrated what we learned from this study into our own projects with increasing success as contractors become more familiar with these "landfill diversion" methods.

Now, as we pen the first pages of the twenty-first century, reducing greenhouse gas emissions has become a significant rallying cry, and recent global droughts and floods have spurred emerging efforts to reduce water consumption in buildings. Considerations long secondary to building design are becoming primary as we challenge each project to be independent of municipal storm sewer systems. Parking areas and roof areas receive attention early in the design process, so we can reduce capital and operational costs. Watching the advent of sodded parking and rooftop gardens, we now know that both can be literally as well as metaphorically green.

As new issues come forward, it's exciting to see how sustainable approaches can flex to meet the need. Each time the lens expands, it becomes clear that the integration used to bring clarity in a narrower field continues to generate solutions that make sense. Sustainable design expands from the question of individual systems to whole buildings, sites, communities and then to the scale of sustainable cities.

Key to bringing those sustainable approaches into the mainstream is demand. But what should owners or tenants or civic-minded voters demand? How can a client be sure a design is sustainable, synergistic, superior? Just as the EnerGuide signals the efficiency of appliances and SPF ratings gauge the protectability of sunscreen, we need a shorthand for identifying high performing buildings.

Tony Grice: This is just the very start of what I call sustainable engineering. We're trying to make systems simpler and work more naturally with the environment rather than throwing a bunch of technology at the building. Chris Jepson: Our ultimate goal is to design a building that does not have a mechanical system, where it's all integral to the building. Grice: … a building that is 100 per cent naturally lit during the day. Jepson: You might think I'm crazy to promote a perfect building without any systems in it. As an engineer, I've just done myself out of a job. But the value I bring to the design is not in how big my boiler is, but what do I contribute to how that building lives.

Legislation — or free market?
What should drive the shift?

Tony Grice: The Europeans are always ahead. That's where all the innovation comes from in terms of product. Being innovative in how you apply it, I think that's what we're good at.

Vivian Manasc: In Europe, sustainability is legislated in, so that becomes the normative price. We're doing the North American version, which is non-legislated, free market, low-budget.

Grice: That's interesting, because I've been dead set against regulating energy efficiency. I saw that as more stifling than actually doing any good, because it seems to me if government sets the limit, then you go through all sorts of hoops and some bureaucratic regulatory process to get there, breathe a sigh of relief and stop. But you're saying if you heavily regulate our industry, it does create innovation.

Manasc: You just raise the bar.

"What we're talking about here is transforming the Canadian market. There are great projects getting designed and built across the country. The goal is to make it business as usual, so it's not dramatic or profound, but to be expected." ~*Kevin Hyde*

Richard Isaac: For example, the new Reichstag in Berlin takes more energy than it's allowed, so they've been using vegetable oil to create heat. So the legislation has created innovation.

Manasc: I actually think regulation is a more effective tool than the marketplace, but regulation that is benchmarked. In other words, regulation that says you get so much energy, not regulation that says this is the type of pump you have to use, or motor, or lights. Some measurable requirement, I believe, does drive innovation, and it drives people to adjust their capital budgets to achieve those things. One of the challenges we have in North America is that our capital budgets are extremely low. When guys from Norway show us what they call low-cost housing, they have capital budgets three times higher than our high-cost housing, so we're not even on the same page.

Grice: I agree with everything you say; engineers would call it system capacity. California has been driving improvements in air quality by what they've been forcing manufacturers to do to automobiles. So that was legislation, and it was one state driving the rest of the world.

Yardsticks.

In Canada, federal programs such as "C2000" and "CBIP" provide marks of excellence, as previous chapters note, but even the more widely known CBIP reaches less than five per cent of the market. Canada is serving as the secretariat for an effort (by the International Initiative for a Sustainable Built Environment) to create an international standard, and some Canadian architects have begun using an adapted form of GreenLeaf, a standard developed in the United Kingdom. Amid the plethora of options, what's emerging as the defacto North American standard is LEED™ (Leadership in Energy and Environmental Design). Developed by the U.S. Green Building Council with broad industry support, this voluntary framework identifies a building as certified, silver, gold or platinum based on points earned on a standard scale. A Canadian version is under development.

"It's hard to tell how good a building is until you do a careful assessment of it. Assessments cost money. So everyone is very busy trying to develop indicators that might explain 80 per cent of performance with 20 per cent of the effort." ~Nils Larsson

Pleased by the momentum toward identifying high performing buildings, I decided to write the LEED™ exam in the summer of 2002, becoming Edmonton's first architect, to achieve this designation. In addition to striving for LEED™ certification, we continue to seek funds under the CBIP program and gauge our work according to C2000 criteria.

Labeling will do its job when owners, both public and private, demand nothing less than certified buildings. Municipalities such as Vancouver, Seattle and Los Angeles already specify that any new building must be "LEED silver," and provinces such as Manitoba are contemplating similar measures.

Those of us spreading the sustainability gospel are fully aware that dollars still drive those decisions, even when social and environmental responsibility plays a role. Thus a clear understanding of savings gained by proven sustainability is key to mainstreaming this agenda, but it's a task complicated by the notoriously volatile nature of construction. Labour, material

Chris Jepson:
With energy costs going up, we can justify doing a lot more. And that's not going to change. So now it's not just something you do because it's right. Why would you want to do anything different? Because if you don't, there's going to be a huge bill. Let alone for environmental reasons.

Tony Grice:
It's going to be legislated. But we're not waiting for that. We want to be on the top of the curve, leading the initiative. Not just sort of mopping up behind.

Vancouver Island Technology Park
LEED Project # 0113
LEED Version 2.0 Certification Level: GOLD
February 3, 2002

41 Points Achieved		Possible Points: **69**

Certified 26 to 32 points   **Silver** 33 to 38 points   **Gold** 39 to 51 points   **Platinum** 52 or more points

10 Sustainable Sites — Possible Points: 14

Y

Y	Prereq 1	Erosion & Sedimentation Control	
1	Credit 1	Site Selection	1
	Credit 2	Urban Redevelopment	1
1	Credit 3	Brownfield Redevelopment	1
1	Credit 4.1	Alternative Transportation, Public Transportation Access	1
1	Credit 4.2	Alternative Transportation, Bicycle Storage & Changing Rooms	1
	Credit 4.3	Alternative Transportation, Alternative Fuel Refueling Stations	1
1	Credit 4.4	Alternative Transportation, Parking Capacity	1
1	Credit 5.1	Reduced Site Disturbance, Protect or Restore Open Space	1
1	Credit 5.2	Reduced Site Disturbance, Development Footprint	1
1	Credit 6.1	Stormwater Management, Rate and Quantity	1
1	Credit 6.2	Stormwater Management, Treatment	1
1	Credit 7.1	Landscape & Exterior Design to Reduce Heat Islands, Nor	1
	Credit 7.2	Landscape & Exterior Design to Reduce Heat Islands, Roc	1
	Credit 8	Light Pollution Reduction	1

4 Water Efficiency — Possible Points: 5

Y

1	Credit 1.1	Water Efficient Landscaping, Reduce by 50%	1
1	Credit 1.2	Water Efficient Landscaping, No Potable Use or No Irrigation	1
	Credit 2	Innovative Wastewater Technologies	1
1	Credit 3.1	Water Use Reduction, 20% Reduction	1
1	Credit 3.2	Water Use Reduction, 30% Reduction	1

6 Energy & Atmosphere — Possible Points: 17

Y

Y	Prereq 1	Fundamental Building Systems Commissioning	
Y	Prereq 2	Minimum Energy Performance	
Y	Prereq 3	CFC Reduction in HVAC&R Equipment	
2	Credit 1.1	Optimize Energy Performance, 20% New / 10% Existing	2
2	Credit 1.2	Optimize Energy Performance, 30% New / 20% Existing	2
2	Credit 1.3	Optimize Energy Performance, 40% New / 30% Existing	2
	Credit 1.4	Optimize Energy Performance, 50% New / 40% Existing	2
	Credit 1.5	Optimize Energy Performance, 60% New / 50% Existing	2
	Credit 2.1	Renewable Energy, 5%	1
	Credit 2.2	Renewable Energy, 10%	1
	Credit 2.3	Renewable Energy, 20%	1
	Credit 3	Additional Commissioning	1
	Credit 4	Ozone Depletion	1
	Credit 5	Measurement & Verification	1
	Credit 6	Green Power	1

7 Materials & Resources — Possible Points: 13

Y

Y	Prereq 1	Storage & Collection of Recyclables	
1	Credit 1.1	Building Reuse, Maintain 75% of Existing Shell	1
	Credit 1.2	Building Reuse, Maintain 100% of Existing Shell	1
	Credit 1.3	Building Reuse, Maintain 100% Shell & 50% Non-Shell	1
1	Credit 1.4	Construction Waste Management, Divert 50%	1
1	Credit 1.5	Construction Waste Management, Divert 75%	1
1	Credit 1.6	Resource Reuse, Specify 5%	1
	Credit 1.7	Resource Reuse, Specify 10%	1
1	Credit 1.8	Recycled Content, Specify 25%	1
	Credit 1.9	Recycled Content, Specify 50%	1
1	Credit 1.10	Local/Regional Materials, 20% Manufactured Locally	1
1	Credit 1.11	Local/Regional Materials, of 20% Above, 50% Harvested Locally	1
	Credit 1.12	Rapidly Renewable Materials	1
	Credit 1.13	Certified Wood	1

9 Indoor Environmental Quality — Possible Points: 15

Y

Y	Prereq 1	Minimum IAQ Performance	
Y	Prereq 2	Environmental Tobacco Smoke (ETS) Control	
1	Credit 1	Carbon Dioxide (CO_2) Monitoring	1
1	Credit 2	Increase Ventilation Effectiveness	1
	Credit 3.1	Construction IAQ Management Plan, During Construction	1
	Credit 3.2	Construction IAQ Management Plan, Before Occupancy	1
1	Credit 4.1	Low-Emitting Materials, Adhesives & Sealants	1
1	Credit 4.2	Low-Emitting Materials, Paints	1
1	Credit 4.3	Low-Emitting Materials, Carpet	1
1	Credit 4.4	Low-Emitting Materials, Composite Wood	1
1	Credit 5	Indoor Chemical & Pollutant Source Control	1
	Credit 6.1	Controllability of Systems, Perimeter	1
	Credit 6.2	Controllability of Systems, Non-Perimeter	1
1	Credit 7.1	Thermal Comfort, Comply with ASHRAE 55-1992	1
	Credit 7.2	Thermal Comfort, Permanent Monitoring System	1
	Credit 8.1	Daylight & Views, Daylight 75% of Spaces	1
1	Credit 8.2	Daylight & Views, Views for 90% of Spaces	1

5 Innovation & Design Process — Possible Points: 5

Y

1	Credit 1.1	Innovation in Design: Construction Waste Management 90%	1
1	Credit 1.2	Innovation in Design: Recycled Content 100%	1
1	Credit 1.3	Innovation in Design: Reuse Historic Building	1
1	Credit 1.4	Innovation in Design: Green Building Demonstration Project	1
1	Credit 2	LEEDô Accredited Professional	1

and energy costs rollercoaster and budgets almost always evolve to encompass unexpected costs, muddying attempts to compare the capital cost of sustainable structures against old-school alternatives. Operating benefits such as comfort and productivity still are seen as different measure, even though they're increasingly widely researched, and ever easier to quantify.

Fortunately, research continues and labeling systems are evolving to reflect regional differences in climate and cost of living, solidifying the evidence that integrated sustainability offers not only operating and environmental benefits, but economies during construction. While some contend we're not yet at the stage where the typical sustainable building costs no more than the typical old-school structure, there's no doubt that integrated design squeezes more value out of each dollar spent.

Energy modeling plays a key role in our integrated design process, prodding us to challenge ingrained "safety factors." At first, it was far more important to ask the questions than to know the answers. Now, as our team builds its ability to fine-tune design in response to the answers generated by simulating a building's performance, our modeling software no longer tells us enough. For example, it doesn't fully account for the benefit of operable windows and natural ventilation; we still check assumptions based on the fact that windows might be closed. New software to model the dynamics of air flow from operable windows is available and should be in more common use within the next few years, part of the increasing sophistication in a tool that informs architecture's unique ability to live on the cusp of art and science.

Factual support for design decisions plus growing recognition of the wisdom of life-cycle costing speed the acceptance of new alternatives among owners, but also among others whose voices hold significant sway—builders, subtrades, cost consultants, maintenance crews, tenants, voters. But there is still a long way to go. I can't help envying European colleagues, many of whom benefit from both legislated energy requirements and construction budgets sharply higher than the Canadian norm. Perhaps it's no wonder that we turn across the pond for prime examples of tomorrow's materials and systems, from high-tech skins to self-adjusting window screens. Would legislation speed our ability to integrate those approaches? I think yes—but legislation keyed to outcomes, not methods.

In the absence of legislation, I remain hopeful that the high-performance buildings sprinkled across Canada are proof enough to convince a skeptic who takes the time to ponder the cycle of life.

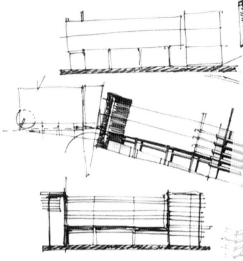

Moving on.

Our next sustainable project is a teaching centre and office building for St. John Ambulance, to be built in Edmonton in 2003. Integrating the design team and the client team from the start, we soon learned that this urban building will be used intensely, daytime and evening. In response, we challenged ourselves to develop an even more sustainable solution than in previous projects, using the LEED^{TM}-silver framework to test an expanded set of strategies. The value of thermal mass, for example, led us to frame this building in concrete rather than wood.

The airy east side of the building is transparent and open to the morning light while the west side features more solid and massive elements, evoking St. John's medieval history. An atrium on the east side acts as an air plenum, providing plenty of vertical space to moderate varied air temperatures. We've taken advantage of the flexibility provided by access flooring for upper level offices, but shift to the linoleum or concrete for the classrooms below, where students will be on the floor practicing their life-saving techniques.

In addition to an even more high-performance envelope than usual, the building will be fitted with operable windows in all classrooms and offices, plus sun-shades and indirect lighting. D-lab, our industrial design team, is researching and refining the design of shading devices to complement this building. Projected energy savings stand at 52 per cent compared to a typical building of this type, providing annual savings of over $20 000 for a 3500m^2 building.

Other elements of this building include its siting near a busy intersection (allowing for good access by bus or bicycle), underground parking, use of native plant material without irrigation and required use of low-emitting paints and adhesives. Daylight penetrates deep into offices with indirect lighting to supplement the design. Capital costs are comparable to school buildings in Edmonton, with mechanical systems proportionately simpler and the building envelope proportionately more effective.

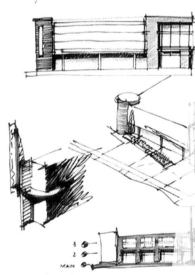

MASSING STUDIES

In the fall of 2002 I find myself travelling across Canada, teaching a Royal Architectural Institute of Canada course on sustainable design with a number of colleagues who are expanding the horizons of sustainable buildings. Joe van Bellengham, a developer in Victoria, has just completed the Vancouver Island Technology Park project. Re-using an abandoned hospital on a rural site, Joe mobilized community support for this conversion to a successful high-tech research park. I'm inspired by the site design with its reduced impact on storm systems, dramatic reductions in water consumption and use of pourous pavements. Joe sought and secured a LEED-Gold rating, partly to help market his building to post-dot-com meltdown tenants.

"The LEED-Gold rating at the Vancouver Island Technology Park has improved marketing and absorption of office space in a very soft real estate market. We've had a lot of free advertising because of our sustainable design strategies." *~Joe Van Bellegham*

Joe's stories illustrate the benefits, both financial and social, of building sustainably. Porous paving systems are now made in Canada. Waterless urinals have been accepted by some municipal authorities. Community groups sometimes support intensive sustainable development. The list goes on.

Another colleague, Wayne Trusty, President of the Athena Sustainable Materials Institute, speaks on the issue of Life Cycle Analysis. As the software becomes more sophisticated, this tool allows design teams to compare the overall environmental impact of all the materials in buildings. Wayne speaks of the importance of this expanded understanding of what's sometimes called "embodied energy," a measure of the overall energy needed to make and transport materials to a building site.

And finally, Bob Charrette and Tim Spiegel speak to the costs of green buildings—Lifecycle Costing and a confirmation of the power of carefully integrated design provide tools to support the business case. Powerful economic arguments for sustainable design complement the environmental and social conversations at sessions from Halifax to Vancouver.

Our newest challenge is the design of the new Government of Canada office building in Yellowknife. Specifically mandated to achieve LEED^{TM}-silver equivalent and set for 2005 completion, this project raises the stakes yet again. Working with our client in the integrated fashion that for us is norm, we are using this project to evolve the expectation of building for the Government of Canada. In addition, results will be closely integrated into design strategies for northern buildings the world over. Among our challenges in this case is the fact that the building will see an evolving list of occupants as federal departments shift. Thus flexibility is key to sustainability in this case; to invite the longest possible life, we must create a structure able to accommodate a wide range of futures.

From the very first, sustainable design discussions are being woven into site planning, building orientation and building form explorations; that integrated approach continues to inform the selection of building systems. Along the way, we are hosting sustainable design "round-tables" with various levels of government, to share and learn from one another.

"There are many thoughts about storytelling and many different kinds of stories to tell...As indigenous cultures know, storytelling is a way to teach and learn over long periods of time. It's a kind of roadmap that passes on the accumulated wisdom about our history and helps us understand unseen parts of the journey." ~*Tom Wujec, Sandra Muscat*

So we continue to write new stories. Stories of the north, of light and darkness, of warm and cold, of places that resonate for people while walking gently on the planet. Our stories are rooted in teaching and in learning, in the joy of shared insights and adventures—and in the pleasures of re-telling.

It's about pulling hard-won knowledge from the fringe into the agora, the place where people are, where economy and ideas connect, where both the idealistic and pragmatic have a voice. It's about demonstrating that, in this case, idealism is in many ways the most pragmatic way. It's about putting the vision of a more sustainable future within people's grasp.

"...only imagination can finally bring

the curtain down.... Imagine a world in

"You must be the change you wish to

which the business of business was to

see in the world."

imagine worlds people might actually

~Mohandes Karamchand Gandhi

want to live in someday. Imagine a world

created by the people, for the people not

perishing from the earth forever. Yeah.

Imagine that." *~Christopher Locke*

After, a look between the lines.

Cheryl: It's appropriate, I think, that a book preaching the power of teamwork reflects the energy of many, including two writers. This being a storybook, perhaps it's also appropriate to share a bit of the saga behind the writing.

Agora Borealis began long ago, gestating in Vivian's brain as she sought a way to transfer an expanding body of work and ideas about sustainable architecture to the printed page. When assenting to serve as scribe and connector of the dots, I warned that my meagre knowledge of the book publishing world would leave gaps in that end of the enterprise. "The right people will appear in our path when we look for them," she said.

Indeed, that's exactly what happened, although not before more than a year (and significant floundering) had passed. It was a fortuitous e-mail to fellow writers that drew Candas Jane Dorsey's interest—and an offer to bring her considerable publishing expertise to the table. With partner Timothy Anderson of The Books Collective, Candas Jane set us on a straightaway course with one magic application of a timeline reminiscent of the Intuit project. Within weeks, Agora Borealis gained a title (thanks, Timothy!) and began appearing in catalogues as the inaugural work of Partners in Design, a sustainable architecture imprint within The Books Collective, with support from the Sustainable Building Consortium and the blessing of consortium partners EPCOR and Keen Engineering.

Anna Coe soon proved another of those "right people" on our path. A newcomer to the Manasc Isaac staff, she plunged into the task of designing this book with admirable flair despite an ever-shrinking timeline. The look and feel of Agora Borealis owes much to her designer's eye—and to her flexibility as new ideas surfaced, complicating life.

As 2002 sped onward, writing accelerated, squeezed between prior commitments in a not-always-seamless flow. More than ever, my family spoke the truth when they said I was often not at home, even when the body was right there, parked in front of the screen. I thank Peter, Reuben, Naomi and Miriam for understanding and merely minor grumbles when served up the leftovers.

At several points in the journey, I struggled with the questions raised by penning a work in two voices. "Where do you want your voice to appear?" Candas asked, in her skillful way of clarifying an action by exposing its roots. Flipping the pages, you see my voice exposed as a sort of bystander's headlamp, peering ahead at what is to come. Equally, though, you've heard it in the weave of voices surrounding Vivian's, shining light from many angles on an ideal that, even if not yet real, can become closer to real by having been put to paper, becoming public in the northern agora.

As in most teams, there were periods of tension. Times when the journalist among us wanted to hang silks on the line to show the layers underpinning a project, only to be told by the architect that, among her colleagues, those would be considered underwear, and politely kept under wraps. It's my hope that we've been courageous enough in showing how these buildings stretch the written and unwritten rules that inevitably surround a profession to inspire you to question how the buildings in your life (including those you sponsor through tax dollars and charitable donations) might become more sustainable. Because truly, this is not simply another litany of words about what is possible, but an unpeeling of what is: tangible evidence that our built landscape can play a significant role in a sustainable future through the synergy of teams who set the bar high—and then clear it.

Works cited.

Boddy, Trevor. "The Architecture of Tourism: Banff Town Hall," Canadian Architect, January 1997.

Calvino, Italo. Invisible Cities. London: Pan Books, 1979.

Cole, Raymond J. Linking and Prioritizing Environmental Criteria: New Agendas, Advanced Buildings Newsletter. Volume I Number 11, January 1996.

Canadian Oxford Dictionary. Don Mills: Oxford University Press Canada, 1998.

CBC Radio. www.cbc.ca (search: Amiskwaciy), Newsworld Feature, June 13, 2002.

Corbett, Michael. Quoted in Green Development: Integrating Ecology & Real Estate. Rocky Mountain Institute: John Wiley & Sons, 1998.

Daly, John. "R.O.B. Magazine's (3rd) annual ranking of Canada's top employers by Hewitt Associates," Report On Business Magazine, Jan. 2002.

Dempster, Mike. "Creative culture fosters winning workplace," Business Edge, Jan. 31-Feb. 6, 2002.

Finlayson, Dave. Edmonton Journal. "Intuit second-best company to work for," January 2001.

Fuller, Buckminster. And It Came to Pass - Not to Stay, New York: MacMillan, 1976.

Jaffe, Nina & Steve Zeitlin. While Standing on One Foot: Puzzle Stories and Wisdom Tales from the Jewish Tradition, Henry Holt & Co., 1996.

Kelly, Tom with Jonathan Littman. The Art of Innovation: Lessons in Creativity from IDEO, America's Leading Design Firm. New York: Doubleday Currency Books, 2001.

Koestler, Arthur. The Sleepwalkers: A History of Man's Changing Vision of the Universe. Hutchison, 1959.

Lasdun, Denys. Architecture in an Age of Scepticism. Heinemann: London, 1984.

MacKenzie, Gordon. Orbiting the Giant Hairball: A Corporate Fool's Guide to Surviving with Grace. New York: Viking Press, 1998.

Mendler, Sandra F. & William Odell. The HOK Guidebook to Sustainable Design. New York: John Wiley & Sons, Inc., 2000.

Mitchell, Alanna. "Cleaning Up: Hot Property," Canadian Living, May 2002.

Pascale, Richard T. , Mark Milleman and Linda Gioja. Surfing The Edge of Chaos, The Laws of Nature and The New Laws of Business. New York: Three Rivers Press, 2000.

Polo, Marco. "Greening Government." Canadian Architect, January 2002.
Saarinen, Eliel. Quoted in Time, July 2, 1956.

Saul, John Ralston. On Equilibrium, Toronto: Penguin, 2001.

Senge, Peter. The Fifth Discipline: The Art and Practice of the Learning Organization. New York: Currency Doubleday, 1990.

Searls, Doc and David Weinberger. The cluetrain manifesto: the end of business as usual. Cambridge: Perseus Publishing, 2001.

Taking Pulse Report, National Aboriginal Achievement Foundation. Proceedings of national forum convened in Calgary, Feb. 6, 2002.

Turchansky, Ray. The Edmonton Journal. "Quick Tax manufacturer builds new call centre," Nov. 9, 2000; "$14M digs for growing software company," Feb. 1, 2002.

Walton, Thomas. Architecture And The Corporation. Simon & Schuster, Inc., 2001.

Wilson, Alex. Environmental Building News. Volume 7, Number 1, January 1998.

Wujec, Tom & Sandra Muscat. Return on Imagination Realizing the Power of Ideas. Toronto: Prentice Hall, 2001.

Zona, Guy A. The Soul would have no rainbow if the eyes had no tears — and other Native American proverbs. New York: Touchstone, 1994.

Voices.

Banff Town Hall: Mile Zero

Architecture:	Vivian Manasc, Jeremy Sturgess, Lesley Beale, Derek Heslop. Emery Yakowich, Bob Horvath
Consultants:	Chris Jepson (mechanical), Tony Grice (electrical), Doug Carlyle (landscape), Reed Ellis (structural)
Client:	Town of Banff – Leslie Taylor (Former Mayor), Doug Leighton (Former Director of Planning), Jim Bennett (Town Manager)
Contractor:	Pentagon Construction
Other voices:	Shafraaz Kaba (student), Kevin Hyde (President, Keen Engineering), Nils Larrson (Program Manager, C-2000 Program for Advanced Commercial Buildings), Cairine MacDonald (President of EPCOR Energy Services)

Hinton Government Centre: A bridge between

Architecture:	Vivian Manasc, Mike Woodland, Derek Heslop, Deana MacKenzie, Emery Yakowich, Werner Jappsen
Consultants:	Tony Grice (electrical), Chris Jepson (mechanical), Gord Shymko (energy modeling), Bob Gibbs (Landscape Architect) Stefan Johanson (Landscape Architect)
Client:	Town of Hinton – Ross Risvold (Former Mayor), Bernie Kreiner (Town Manager), Dale Rhyason (Town Engineer), Dwayne Breitkruitz (Development Information Officer), Lorne Stadnick (Former Director of Engineering and Development)
Contractor:	Graham Construction, Grant Beck (Project Manager)

Intuit: A place to call home

Architecture: Vivian Manasc, Wes Sims, Emery Yakowich, Deana MacKenzie, Sandra Valens, Jack McCutcheon

Consultants: Chris Jepson (mechanical), Tony Grice (electrical), Doug Carlyle (Landscape Architect), Martin Gillet (civil)

Client: Intuit Canada - Bruce Johnson (Founder and President), Chad Frederick (Vice President), Nimal Rodrigo (Controller), Cheryll Watson (Facilities Manager)

Contractor: Clark Builders - Bill Giebelhaus (Partner), Brian Robinson (Vice President, Business Development), Terry Richelhoff (Project Manager), Dave Wardrop (Project Superintendent), Kevin Nelson (Assistant Superintendent), Aftab Jessa (Estimator)

Other voices: Atan Das (Owner's Agent), Garry Stebner (President, Consor Developers)

Amisckwaciy Academy: Raising the Bar

Architecture: Richard Isaac, Vivian Manasc, Shafraaz Kaba, Deana Mackenzie, Jack McCutcheon

Consultants: David Brown (Landscape Architect), Chris Jepson (mechanical), Tony Grice (electrical)

Client: Edmonton Public Schools - Angus McBeath (Superintendent), Phyllis Cardinal (Principal, Amiskwaciy Academy), Gary Holroyd (Project Manager), Roland Labbe (Planner), Brian Fedor (Managing Director, Facilities Services), Shirly McNeill (Assistant Principal, Amiskwaciy Academy)

Contractor: Cavan Contractors Ltd., Jack Jones (Project Manager)

Other voices: Mark Kolke (Realtor, Colliers International Inc.), Lyle Oberg (Alberta Minister of Learning), Nicole Sharphead and Kimberly Baptiste (students, Amiskwaciy Academy), John Kim Bell (Founder and President, National Aboriginal Achievement Foundation)

Photo & drawing credits.

The following photographers and artists created the images in this book. All photos and drawings are copyright by Manasc Isaac Architects unless noted below.

Drawings

© Lesley Beale
    page 20
© Myron Nebozuk
    page 162
© Sturgess Architects
    page 24
© Marat Feldman
    page 138

Photography

© Jim Dow
    pages 51 (bottom right), 55, 58, 59, 60, 72, 73, 74,
    83, 84, 88, 89, 91, 94, 101, 114 (left & centre), 117
© Elaine Gottlieb
    pages 95. 96, 118
© Robert Lemermeyer
    page 18, 19, 20, 21, 26, 37
© Sonny Shem
    pages 44, 45, 48, 139, 142, 145